christmas

FEASTS and TREATS

CHRISTMAS FEASTS AND TREATS

Copyright © Donna Hay Pty Ltd 2018, 2022
Design copyright © Donna Hay Pty Ltd 2018, 2022
Photography copyright © Chris Court, Ben Dearnley, William Meppem, Con Poulos, Anson Smart
Author: Donna Hay
Art direction and design: Chi Lam
Art director and managing editor: Hannah Schubert
Copy editors: Abby Pfahl and Mariam Digges
Recipes and styling: Donna Hay, Steve Pearce, Justine Poole, Tina McLeish, Jacinta Cannataci,
Jessica Brook, Georgina Esdaile, Amber De Florio, Dolores Braga Menéndez, Hayley Dodd
dh Digital strategist and producer: Lauren Gibb
dh Brand and partnerships manager: Rebecca Jones

Fourth Estate
An imprint of HarperCollins*Publishers*

HarperCollins*Publishers*
Australia • Brazil • Canada • France • Germany • Holland • Hungary
India • Italy • Japan • Mexico • New Zealand • Poland • Spain • Sweden
Switzerland • United Kingdom • United States of America

First published in Australia and New Zealand in 2018
This revised and expanded edition published in 2022
by HarperCollinsPublishers Australia Pty Limited
Level 13, 201 Elizabeth Street, Sydney NSW 2000
ABN 36 009 913 517
harpercollins.com.au

A catalogue record for this book is available from the National Library of Australia
ISBN 978 1 4607 6237 0

On the cover: Christmas wreath, photographed by Con Poulos

Reproduction by News PreMedia Centre, Splitting Image and Hannah Schubert
Printed and bound in China by RR Donnelley on 128gsm matt artpaper
6 5 4 3 2   23 24 25 26

christmas
FEASTS and TREATS

FOURTH ESTATE

contents

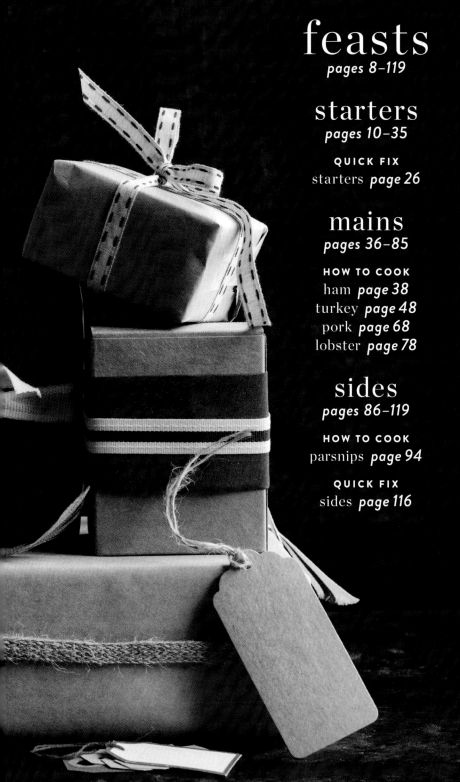

introduction

Christmas at my house usually consists of my three favourite things – family, laughter and, let's be honest, a little craziness. My boys wake up super early (of course!) so, after a few presents, it's become a ritual of ours to dash down for a swim in the ocean. Refreshed and salty, we head home to get ready for lunch, and it's not long before I'm prepping canapés in the kitchen with my sisters and a glass of Champagne. It's these kinds of moments I think we all treasure on Christmas Day. Don't get me wrong, I have quite the weakness for festive food and all its trimmings, but I'm also really into finding new ways to dial down the entertaining stress and make more room for fun. This book has all my fuss-free tips, styling tricks and, most importantly, stunning but simple recipes you can count on for the big day. It's my way of wishing you a very happy (and relaxed!) Christmas.

feasts

I know some of you celebrate with an enchanting dinner on Christmas Eve, and some will be hosting a long lunch on the day itself. Maybe you're a guest this year and you've been asked to bring something? You'll find all things savoury to feast on here. There's inspiration for starters and sides, plus step-by-step guides to walk you through the big four: glazed ham, succulent turkey, roast pork and grilled lobster. Keep an eye out for my tips and shortcuts, like my glossy cheat's ham that doesn't require basting every 10 minutes, and turkey that cooks gently on the stovetop (in less than an hour!), leaving room for ham and vegetables in the oven below.

starters

'Tis the season for zingy seafood snacks, punchy pass-abouts and dreamy dips. These low-lift crowd-pleasers sing with flavour and skimp on fuss, guaranteed to spread Christmas cheer. All that's left to do is spin the carols and pour the fizz.

brie and caramelised onion tarts

brie and caramelised onion tarts

60g unsalted butter
4 onions, thinly sliced
1½ tablespoons caster (superfine) sugar
¼ cup (60ml) white wine vinegar
¼ cup rosemary leaves, plus 12 x 4cm sprigs extra
sea salt and cracked black pepper
750g store-bought ready-rolled butter puff pastry
2 egg yolks
¾ cup (180ml) pure cream
150g triple cream brie, sliced into 12 pieces

Preheat oven to 180°C (350°F). Lightly grease
12 x ⅓-cup-capacity (80ml) muffin tins.
   Melt the butter in a large non-stick frying pan over
medium heat. Add the onion, cover with a tight-fitting
lid and cook for 10 minutes. Add the sugar, vinegar,
rosemary, salt and pepper and cook, uncovered,
for 5 minutes or until the onion is golden brown.
   Using a cookie cutter, cut 12 x 10cm rounds from
the pastry and press them into the prepared tins.
   Place the egg yolks and cream in a small bowl and
whisk to combine. Spoon the caramelised onion into
the tart bases and pour the egg mixture over them.
Place a piece of brie on top of each and bake for
35 minutes or until puffed and golden. Top each tart
with a rosemary sprig and serve warm. MAKES 12
Tip: Lightly dust the pastry with plain flour to make
handling easier.

prosciutto crostini with pickled cherries

3 cups (450g) frozen pitted cherries
1 teaspoon juniper berries, lightly crushed
¾ cup (180ml) balsamic vinegar
¼ cup (60g) firmly packed brown sugar
sea salt and cracked black pepper
8 slices ciabatta or baguette
extra virgin olive oil, for brushing
150g triple cream brie, sliced into 8 pieces
8 slices prosciutto

Place the cherries, juniper, balsamic, brown sugar, salt and
pepper in a medium frying pan over high heat and bring
to the boil. Reduce the heat to a simmer and cook for
15–20 minutes or until the cherries are soft and the liquid
is syrupy. Set aside.
   Preheat a char-grill pan over medium heat. Brush the
bread slices with oil and cook for 2 minutes each side or
until charred.
   To assemble, spoon the pickled cherries onto the charred
bread and top with a slice each of brie and prosciutto. SERVES 4
+ Store the pickled cherries in an airtight container in the
refrigerator for up to 3 weeks.

warm lemon olives

½ cup (125ml) extra virgin olive oil+
2 tablespoons shredded lemon rind
1 tablespoon lemon thyme leaves
½ teaspoon cracked black pepper
1 small red chilli, halved
400g green olives
1 tablespoon lemon juice

Place a medium frying pan over low heat. Add the oil,
lemon rind, lemon thyme, pepper and chilli and cook for
3–4 minutes.
   Add the olives and gently stir to coat. Cook for
3 minutes or until warmed through. Add the lemon juice
and stir to combine. Serve warm. MAKES 2½ CUPS
+ Use a good-quality fruity olive oil for this recipe, if you can.

warm lemon olives

prosciutto crostini with pickled cherries

2 bunches baby beetroot (about 8 beetroots), scrubbed
    and thinly sliced using a mandoline, small leaves reserved
50g baby beetroot leaves
red-veined sorrel, to serve
oat pastry
1 cup (90g) rolled oats
¼ cup (50g) white chia seeds
½ teaspoon fine table salt
1 cup (120g) wholemeal (whole-wheat) spelt flour
½ cup (60g) almond meal (ground almonds)
⅓ cup (80ml) light-flavoured extra virgin olive oil
2 tablespoons water
1 egg
whipped feta
150g soft feta
⅓ cup (80g) sour cream
¼ teaspoon Dijon mustard
beetroot dressing
1 tablespoon light-flavoured extra virgin olive oil
1 tablespoon red wine vinegar
1 teaspoon finely grated orange rind
sea salt and cracked black pepper

salt in a food processor and process for 1 minute or until
the mixture resembles fine breadcrumbs. Add the flour
and almond meal and pulse to combine.

Place the oil, water and egg in a small jug and whisk to
combine. With the motor running, gradually pour the oil
mixture into the oat mixture, processing until combined
but still crumbly. Divide the dough into 2 portions.

Roll each portion out between 2 sheets of non-stick
baking paper to make 2 rough 15cm x 36cm rectangles.
Remove the top sheet of baking paper from each dough
portion and place them on separate baking trays. Bake for
5–7 minutes or until golden and crisp. Allow to cool
completely on the trays.

To make the whipped feta, place the feta, sour cream
and mustard in a bowl and whisk to combine. Set aside.

To make the beetroot dressing, combine the oil, vinegar,
orange rind, salt and pepper in a large bowl.

Add the beetroot to the dressing and toss to coat.

To assemble, place the oat pastry on serving platters
and top with the whipped feta, beetroot, beetroot leaves
and red-veined sorrel. Drizzle with any remaining beetroot
dressing, sprinkle with pepper and serve. SERVES 6–8

beetroot tart with whipped feta

beetroot-cured ocean trout

beetroot-cured ocean trout

1 x 400g piece sashimi-grade ocean trout, skin removed
   and pin-boned
¾ cup (185g) crème fraîche
2 teaspoons store-bought grated horseradish[+]
1 sourdough baguette, thinly sliced and toasted
2 bulbs baby fennel (260g), trimmed and thinly sliced
   using a mandoline
store-bought pickled red onions, to serve
micro (baby) flat-leaf parsley leaves[++] (optional), to serve
sea salt and cracked black pepper, for sprinkling
beetroot curing mixture
2 tablespoons black peppercorns, lightly crushed
3 large beetroots (600g), peeled and coarsely grated
½ cup chopped dill leaves
1.2kg rock salt
1 cup (220g) caster (superfine) sugar

To make the beetroot curing mixture, place the pepper,
beetroot, dill, salt and sugar in a large bowl and mix to
combine. Spread half the beetroot curing mixture into the
base of a glass or ceramic baking dish. Top with the trout and
the remaining curing mixture to coat. Cover with plastic
wrap, top with a small tray and weigh down with 2–3 tin cans
or a heavy saucepan. Refrigerate for 4 hours (but no longer).

   Remove the trout from the beetroot curing mixture and
use a pastry brush to brush away any remaining salt. Use a
sharp knife to thinly slice the trout.

   Mix the crème fraîche and the horseradish in a small
bowl to combine.

   Top the baguette slices with a little of the crème fraîche
mixture, fennel, trout, pickled onion and micro parsley.
Sprinkle with salt and pepper to serve. **SERVES 4 AS A STARTER**
+ *You can buy ready-grated horseradish in jars at supermarkets*
and greengrocers.
++ *Micro herbs are available from greengrocers, farmers'*
markets and select supermarkets. If you can't find any, use
regular herbs.
Tip: The cured trout will keep, tightly covered in plastic wrap,
in the refrigerator for up to 3 days.

lobster roll

¼ cup (75g) whole-egg mayonnaise
1 teaspoon finely grated lemon rind
2 tablespoons extra virgin olive oil
1 long red chilli, thinly sliced
4 bao buns[+], steamed
1 cup celery leaves
150g cooked lobster tail (about 1 small tail)[++],
   meat sliced
sea salt flakes

Combine the mayonnaise and lemon rind in a small bowl.
Set aside.

   Heat the oil in a small frying pan over medium heat.
Add the chilli and cook for 3–4 minutes or until crisp.

   Spread the lemon mayonnaise inside each bun and top
with some celery leaves, lobster, crisp chilli and salt flakes,
before serving. **MAKES 4**
+ *Bao buns are available from select supermarkets and Asian*
grocers. Steam following the packet instructions.
++ *You can buy cooked lobster meat from your fishmonger.*
Tip: If you prefer, swap out the lobster for 8 large peeled,
cleaned and cooked king prawns (shrimp).

Luxe meets low-fuss with these seafood stars.
Dialed up with my *flavour shortcuts* and a generous
pinch of fun, they're sure to get the party started!

Although I love *a big family lunch*, it's those *more intimate gatherings* that allow me to create something *a little bit special* like these *upscaled lobster bao buns.*

lobster roll

crab pasta with sourdough crunch

crab pasta with sourdough crunch

400g dried angel hair pasta or thin spaghetti
2 tablespoons extra virgin olive oil
2 cloves garlic, thinly sliced
2 long red chillies, thinly sliced
2 teaspoons finely grated lemon rind
¼ cup (60ml) dry white wine
400g cooked picked blue swimmer or spanner crab
 meat, plus extra crab legs[+] to serve
¼ cup (60ml) lemon juice
red-veined sorrel, to serve
sourdough crunch
2 tablespoons extra virgin olive oil
1 clove garlic, crushed
sea salt and cracked black pepper
1 cup (70g) fresh sourdough breadcrumbs

To make the sourdough crunch, place the oil, garlic and
salt in a medium frying pan over medium heat and cook
for 1 minute or until the garlic is soft. Add the breadcrumbs
and cook, stirring, for 10 minutes or until the crumbs are
golden. Set aside.
 Cook the pasta in a large saucepan of boiling salted
water for 8 minutes or until al dente. Drain and set aside.
 Place the oil, garlic, chilli and lemon rind in a large
non-stick frying pan over medium heat and cook for
2 minutes or until the garlic is soft. Pour in the wine and
cook for 2 minutes. Add the crab meat, pasta, lemon
juice, salt and pepper and toss to combine. Divide the
pasta between bowls and top with the sourdough crunch,
the extra crab legs and red-veined sorrel.
SERVES 6 AS A STARTER
*+ You can buy cooked picked crab meat and legs from
your fishmonger.*

coconut chicken summer rolls

400g cooked chicken, finely shredded
8 x 16cm rice paper rounds
2 cups mizuna[+] or Asian leaves
1 cup mint leaves
1 cup coriander (cilantro) leaves
4 green onions (scallions), thinly sliced
4 radishes, thinly sliced
½ cup micro (baby) shiso leaves[++]
coconut dressing
200ml coconut cream
2 tablespoons lime juice
1 tablespoon fish sauce
1 teaspoon caster (superfine) sugar

To make the coconut dressing, place the coconut cream,
lime juice, fish sauce and sugar in a bowl and mix to combine.
 Place the chicken and half the coconut dressing in a
bowl and mix to combine.
 To assemble the rolls, place 1 rice paper round in a bowl
of lukewarm water for 10 seconds or until slightly softened.
Transfer to a clean damp tea towel and place a little of the
mizuna, mint, coriander, coconut chicken, green onion,
radish and shiso leaves down the centre of the round.
Fold over 2 short ends, then fold the two long sides
over to secure the filling and roll up tightly to enclose.
Repeat with the remaining ingredients to make 8 rolls.
 Serve with the remaining coconut dressing for dipping.
MAKES 8
*+ Mizuna is also known as Japanese mustard greens and has
a slightly peppery flavour. You can find it in Asian grocers or
select greengrocers.*
*++ Baby shiso leaves are available from select greengrocers
and farmers' markets.*

Filled with fresh herbs and coconut chicken, these summer rolls
make *a light and zingy starter.* They're equally delicious *with
tofu for a vegie alternative* or with cooked and halved prawns.

coconut chicken summer rolls

hot smoked cured salmon

hot smoked cured salmon

1 x 1.2kg salmon fillet, skin removed and pin-boned
1 x 18cm x 50cm cedar grilling plank, soaked in water[+]
12 sprigs dill
½ cup (180g) honey
1 teaspoon dried chilli flakes
cracked black pepper
curing mixture
¾ cup (255g) sea salt flakes
1 cup (240g) firmly packed brown sugar
2 teaspoons dried chilli flakes
horseradish crème fraîche
1¼ cups (310g) crème fraîche
¼ cup finely chopped flat-leaf parsley leaves
1½ tablespoons store-bought grated horseradish (see *note*, page 19)
1½ tablespoons salted capers, rinsed and finely chopped
2 teaspoons finely grated lemon rind

To make the curing mixture, combine the salt, sugar and chilli.
Place one-third of the curing mixture into a large shallow glass
dish. Place the salmon over it and top with the remaining curing
mixture to coat. Refrigerate for 3–4 hours[++].

Rinse the salmon to remove the curing mixture and pat dry with
absorbent kitchen paper. Transfer to a wire rack set over a large
tray and refrigerate, uncovered, for 1 hour or overnight, until the
salmon is completely dry.

Preheat a barbecue grill over medium-high heat. Place the dill
sprigs down the length of the grilling plank. Top with the dried
cured salmon. Combine the honey, chilli and pepper in a small
bowl and brush the mixture over the salmon. Place the plank with
the salmon on the barbecue grill, cover with the lid and cook for
20 minutes or until medium-rare and golden, checking the salmon
constantly and spritzing the plank (not the salmon) with water if
it catches alight[+++].

To make the horseradish crème fraîche, combine the crème
fraîche, parsley, horseradish, capers and lemon rind.

Serve the salmon on the plank (ensure the plank is no longer
smouldering), or transfer to a serving platter, with the horseradish
crème fraîche. **SERVES 8**

*+ You can find cedar grilling planks at hardware stores and barbecue
suppliers. Soak for at least 1 hour before using.*
*++ Cured unsmoked salmon can keep, uncovered, in the refrigerator
for up to 2 days.*
*+++ Have a spray bottle filled with water on hand to put out any
flare-ups on the plank – you want the plank to smoke but without
any flames.*

smoked salmon, wasabi and radish finger sandwiches

250g cream cheese, softened
2 teaspoons wasabi paste
2 teaspoons finely grated lime rind
8 thick slices white bread
4 radishes (150g), trimmed and thinly sliced
8 slices (250g) smoked salmon
micro (baby) shiso leaves (optional) (see *note*, page 22),
   to serve
cracked black pepper, to serve

Place the cream cheese, wasabi and lime rind in a small
bowl and mix to combine.
   Spread two-thirds of the mixture onto the bread slices.
Cover 4 of the bread slices with the radish and top with the
remaining bread, cream cheese-side down. Spread the top
of each sandwich with the remaining cream cheese mixture.
Place 2 slices of the salmon on each sandwich. Trim the
crusts and slice each sandwich into 3 lengths.
   Sprinkle with shiso leaves and pepper to serve. MAKES 12

smoked salmon, mascarpone and tarragon pâté

1 cup (250g) mascarpone
⅓ cup tarragon leaves
1 tablespoon Dijon mustard
1 teaspoon finely grated lemon rind
1 tablespoon lemon juice
cracked black pepper, for sprinkling
300g smoked salmon, chopped
salmon roe, to serve
store-bought seeded crackers, to serve

Place the mascarpone, tarragon, mustard, lemon rind,
lemon juice and pepper in a food processor and process
until smooth. Add the salmon and pulse until just combined.
Divide between serving bowls or sterilised jars and top with
salmon roe.
   Serve the pâté with seeded crackers. SERVES 6
Tip: This pâté will keep refrigerated for 2–3 days.

prawns with bloody mary mayonnaise and celery salt

1kg cooked prawns (shrimp), shells intact
celery salt+, to serve
bloody mary mayonnaise
1 cup (300g) whole-egg mayonnaise
1½ tablespoons tomato sauce (ketchup)
2 teaspoons Tabasco sauce
2 teaspoons Worcestershire sauce
sea salt and cracked black pepper
2 stalks celery, trimmed and finely chopped

To make the bloody mary mayonnaise, place the mayonnaise, tomato sauce, Tabasco sauce, Worcestershire sauce, salt and pepper in a small bowl and mix to combine. Top with the celery.

Place the prawns on a serving plate, sprinkle with the celery salt and serve with the bloody mary mayonnaise.
SERVES 4
+ *Find celery salt in supermarkets or make your own with 1 teaspoon celery seeds and 1 tablespoon sea salt flakes.*
Tip: You can serve the prawns on a bed of crushed ice, if you like.

spicy tabasco lobster sliders

¼ teaspoon dried chilli flakes
1 teaspoon sea salt flakes
¼ cup (75g) whole-egg mayonnaise
2 tablespoons tomato sauce (ketchup)
1 teaspoon Tabasco sauce
1 teaspoon Worcestershire sauce
300g cooked lobster meat (see *note*, page 19), chopped
8 small brioche slider buns, halved
micro (baby) mint leaves (optional)
   (see *note*, page 19), to serve

Place the chilli and salt in a small bowl and mix to combine. Set aside.

Place the mayonnaise, tomato sauce, Tabasco sauce, Worcestershire sauce and lobster in a medium bowl and mix to combine. Divide the lobster mixture between the bun bases, top with the mint and sprinkle with the chilli salt. Sandwich with the bun tops to serve. MAKES 8

ginger, soy and mirin oysters

¼ cup (60ml) mirin (Japanese rice wine)
2 teaspoons soy sauce
1 teaspoon sesame oil
1 tablespoon rice wine vinegar
1 teaspoon lime juice
1 teaspoon finely grated ginger
12 oysters, freshly shucked
black sesame seeds, toasted, to serve
micro (baby) shiso leaves (optional)
  (see *note*, page 22), to serve
lime wedges, to serve

Place the mirin, soy, sesame oil, vinegar, lime juice
and ginger in a small bowl and whisk to combine.
  Place the oysters on a serving plate and spoon
the dressing on top. Sprinkle with the sesame seeds
and shiso and serve with lime wedges. MAKES 12
*Tip: You can serve the oysters on a bed of crushed ice,
if you like.*

tarragon crab cakes with aioli

500g cooked picked crab meat (see *note*, page 22)
1½ cups (100g) fresh sourdough breadcrumbs
1 teaspoon finely grated lemon rind
2 tablespoons finely chopped flat-leaf parsley leaves
2 tablespoons finely chopped tarragon leaves
¼ cup (75g) store-bought aioli, plus extra to serve
sea salt and cracked black pepper
¼ cup (60ml) vegetable oil
watercress sprigs, to serve

Place the crab, breadcrumbs, lemon rind, parsley, tarragon,
aioli, salt and pepper in a large bowl and mix well to combine.
Shape ⅓-cup portions of the mixture into patties.
  Heat the oil in a large non-stick frying pan over medium
heat. Cook the crab cakes in batches for 3 minutes each
side or until golden and crisp. Sprinkle with pepper and
serve with watercress and extra aioli. MAKES 8

ricotta and pea tartlets

6 small flatbreads
2 tablespoons extra virgin olive oil, for brushing
2 cups (480g) fresh ricotta
1 teaspoon finely grated lemon rind
sea salt and cracked black pepper
1 cup (120g) frozen peas, blanched
1 cup snow pea (mange tout) tendrils

Preheat oven to 180°C (350°F). Using an 11cm round cutter, cut 6 rounds from the flatbreads and gently peel to separate each round in half. Brush both sides of the flatbreads with the oil and press into 12 x ½-cup-capacity (125ml) muffin tins to line. Bake for 4–6 minutes or until crisp and golden. Allow to cool in the tins for 5 minutes before removing.

Place the ricotta, lemon rind, salt and pepper in a medium bowl and mix to combine. Place the peas in a small bowl and gently mash with a fork.

Divide the ricotta mixture between the tartlets and top with the peas, snow pea tendrils, salt and pepper to serve.
MAKES 12

smoked salmon and avocado rice paper rolls

8 x 16cm rice paper rounds
8 slices (250g) smoked salmon
1 carrot, peeled and shredded
1 cucumber, shredded
1 avocado, thinly sliced
½ cup coriander (cilantro) leaves
black sesame seeds, to serve
micro (baby) mint leaves (optional)
  (see *note*, page 19), to serve
store-bought pickled chilli+, to serve

Place 1 rice paper round in a large bowl of lukewarm water for 10 seconds or until slightly softened. Transfer to a clean, damp tea towel. Place 1 slice of the salmon in the centre of the round, top with a little of the carrot, cucumber, avocado and coriander and roll to enclose. Repeat with the remaining ingredients to make 8 rolls.

Cut the rolls in half and sprinkle with sesame seeds and mint. Serve with pickled chilli. **MAKES 16**
+ *Pickled chilli is available from Asian grocers.*

hummus with spiced crispy chickpeas

hummus with spiced crispy chickpeas

micro (baby) coriander (cilantro) leaves (optional)
  (see *note*, page 19), to serve
store-bought grissini (bread sticks), to serve
lemon wedges, to serve
spiced crispy chickpeas
¼ cup (50g) white rice flour
2 teaspoons sweet smoked paprika, plus extra for sprinkling
2 teaspoons ground coriander
1 x 400g can chickpeas (garbanzo beans), rinsed and drained
vegetable oil, for shallow frying
hummus
2 x 400g cans chickpeas (garbanzo beans), rinsed
  and drained
2 tablespoons hulled tahini
1 clove garlic, crushed
⅓ cup (80ml) lemon juice
¼ cup (60ml) extra virgin olive oil, plus extra to serve
sea salt and cracked black pepper
2 tablespoons water

To make the hummus, place the chickpeas, tahini, garlic,
lemon juice, olive oil, salt and pepper in a food processor
and process until smooth. Add the water to thin the
hummus if necessary, processing to combine. Refrigerate
for 1 hour or until chilled.

  To make the spiced crispy chickpeas, place the flour,
paprika and ground coriander in a medium bowl and mix to
combine. Add the chickpeas and toss to coat. Heat 1cm of
vegetable oil in a large non-stick frying pan over medium
heat. Cook the chickpeas, in batches, for 4–5 minutes
or until crisp and golden. Drain on absorbent kitchen paper
and sprinkle with salt, pepper and the extra paprika.

  Spoon the hummus onto a serving plate and top with
the crispy chickpeas. Drizzle with the extra oil, sprinkle
with coriander leaves and pepper and serve with grissini
and lemon wedges. MAKES 2½ CUPS

minted spinach dip with yoghurt

500g baby spinach leaves
½ cup (80g) almonds, toasted
3 cups mint leaves
1 tablespoon finely grated lemon rind
1 tablespoon lemon juice
sea salt and cracked black pepper
1 cup (280g) plain thick yoghurt, plus extra to serve
2 tablespoons extra virgin olive oil
micro (baby) basil leaves (optional) (see *note*, page 19),
  to serve
store-bought lavosh crackers, to serve

Blanch the spinach, in batches, in a large saucepan of salted
boiling water for 30 seconds–1 minute or until wilted.
Refresh in iced water and drain well.

  Place the almonds in a food processor and process until
fine. Add the spinach, mint, lemon rind and juice, salt and
pepper and process until smooth. Add the yoghurt and oil and
process to combine. Refrigerate for 1 hour or until chilled.

  Spoon the dip onto a serving plate and top with extra
yoghurt and micro basil. Serve with crackers. MAKES 3 CUPS

minted spinach dip with yoghurt

tuna dip with dukkah

tuna dip with dukkah

1 x 185g can tuna in chilli oil, drained and oil reserved
3 white anchovy fillets
250g cream cheese, chopped
2 tablespoons lemon juice
2 tablespoons extra virgin olive oil
sea salt and cracked black pepper
store-bought dukkah[+], for sprinkling
sourdough baguette, to serve
lemon wedges, to serve

Place the tuna, anchovies, cream cheese, lemon juice,
olive oil, salt and pepper in a food processor and process,
scraping down the sides of the bowl, for 3–4 minutes
or until smooth. Refrigerate for 1 hour or until chilled.
  Spoon the dip onto a serving plate, drizzle with the
reserved chilli oil and sprinkle with the dukkah. Serve with
sourdough bread and lemon wedges. **MAKES 2½ CUPS**
*+ Dukkah is a Middle-Eastern nut and spice blend, available
from spice shops, delicatessens, greengrocers and most
supermarkets. Sprinkle it on meats and salads or use it in
a spice crust.*

labne with pistachios and pomegranate

1 teaspoon sea salt flakes
1kg plain thick yoghurt
2 tablespoons extra virgin olive oil, plus extra to serve
5 sprigs marjoram
seeds and juice from 1 pomegranate
2 tablespoons slivered pistachios
store-bought lavosh crackers or flatbreads, to serve

Add the salt to the yoghurt and mix to combine. Place in
a bowl lined with a double layer of muslin and gather up the
edges to enclose. Suspend the yoghurt from a shelf in the
refrigerator, placing a bowl underneath to collect moisture,
for 24 hours or until the mixture is firm. Unwrap the labne
from the muslin and spoon onto a serving plate.
  Heat the oil in a small non-stick frying pan over medium
heat. Cook the marjoram, in batches, for 30 seconds or
until just crispy. Drain on absorbent kitchen paper.
  Drizzle the labne with the extra oil and 2 tablespoons of
the pomegranate juice. Sprinkle with the pomegranate seeds
and pistachios. Top with the crispy marjoram and serve with
crackers. **MAKES 2½ CUPS**
*Tips: Keep labne refrigerated in an airtight container for up
to 1 week. When frying herbs in oil, make sure they are dry
to start with – this will help prevent the oil from spitting.*

Making your own dip is easier than you think and
pays off big in the *flavour stakes*. Just add your favourite
dippy accompaniments for *crunchy, creamy yum!*

labne with pistachios and pomegranate

mains

My upflavoured spins on all the classics are peppered with shortcuts to make light work of the main event. From sticky hams to juicy birds, and the perfect crackle – plus my secret styling tips for extra wow – these dishes will steal the show.

score the rind

gently pull it back

remove the rind

wrap the hock

pour the glaze over the ham

cheat's glazed ham

3 cups (750ml) fresh orange juice
3 cups (720g) firmly packed brown sugar
1 cup (250ml) red wine vinegar
1 stick cinnamon
8 cloves
16 sprigs thyme
3 cups (750ml) port
1 x 6–7kg ham leg+

Place the juice, sugar, vinegar, cinnamon, cloves and thyme in a medium saucepan over high heat and stir until the sugar has dissolved. Bring to the boil and cook for 30 minutes or until reduced. Remove from the heat, add the port and stir to combine. Strain the glaze into a heatproof jug, discarding the solids.

Preheat oven to 220°C (425°F).

Use a sharp knife to score the skin around the sides and hock of the ham, before using your fingers to gently remove the rind. Trim any excess fat. Wrap the hock of the ham with non-stick baking paper followed by aluminium foil. Pour the glaze into a deep-sided roasting pan. Carefully place the ham, top-side down, into the pan and brush with the glaze. Roast for 40 minutes. Remove from the oven and reduce the oven temperature to 200°C (400°F). Turn the ham over, brush with the glaze and roast for a further 20–25 minutes or until golden.

Remove the ham from the pan and place on a large serving platter. Brush the remaining glaze over the ham before carving (see cook's tips, page 41) to serve. SERVES 12–14
+ This recipe calls for a whole leg of ham, with the bone in, that has been pre-cured and pre-cooked. If you can't buy a pre-cooked ham in your part of the world (sometimes the case in the UK), ask your local butcher for a cured leg and follow their cooking instructions before glazing.

cheat's glazed ham

○ Before serving the ham, remove the foil and paper that cover the hock. Wrap with calico and tie with ribbon for a festive touch.

cook's tips

○ This clever glazed ham is super-simple to prepare but retains the sticky-sweet depth of flavour that defines traditional Christmas ham. There's no need for fussy scoring or studding with tiny cloves, just remove the skin and pour over the warm spiced glaze. The ham will bathe in a generous amount of the glaze while it's in the oven, eliminating the need for persistent basting and ensuring the ham stays moist.

○ When purchasing your ham, be sure to buy a cooked, cured leg.

○ It's not very often that an entire leg of ham is devoured on Christmas day. This, of course, means ham sandwiches all-round for days to follow. Ham will keep longer if it's on the bone, so only slice as much as you need and store the rest in the fridge.

○ Keep the leg of ham fresh in the fridge by covering it in a clean ham bag or tea towel that's been soaked in 2 parts water and 1 part white vinegar. Ensure the bag has been well wrung out before placing it over the ham and refrigerating. Repeat the process with the water and vinegar every 3 days. The ham should last for up to 2 weeks.

carving ham

YOU WILL NEED
a wooden chopping board
a damp tea towel
a large cook's knife

step 1

1. It helps to have some baking paper or calico fastened over the hock of the ham so you can hold it securely while you're carving. Place the chopping board on top of the tea towel to prevent it from moving. Starting at the front of the ham, slice on a slight angle down to the bone.

step 2

2. Run the knife lengthways along the bone to remove the slices. When one-third of the ham has been sliced, remove the bone, cutting it at the joint.

double-glazed juniper ham

double-glazed juniper ham

1 x 6–7kg ham leg (see *note*, page 38)
juniper glaze
1.25 litres fresh orange juice
1¼ cups (310ml) white wine vinegar
1 cup (250ml) tonic water
½ cup (125ml) gin
1.2kg firmly packed brown sugar
2 tablespoons juniper berries
6 bay leaves
8 sprigs lemon thyme

To make the juniper glaze, place the juice, vinegar, tonic, gin, sugar, juniper berries, bay leaves and lemon thyme in a saucepan over high heat. Stir until the sugar is dissolved. Bring to the boil and cook, stirring occasionally, for 30 minutes or until reduced by a third. Strain the glaze into a jug, reserving the juniper berries. Set aside.

Preheat oven to 220°C (425°F).

Use a sharp knife to score the skin around the sides and hock of the ham, before using your fingers to gently remove the rind. Trim any excess fat. Wrap the hock of the ham with non-stick baking paper, then aluminium foil. Pour the glaze into a deep-sided roasting pan. Carefully place the ham, top-side down, into the pan and brush with the glaze. Roast for 30 minutes.

Remove from the oven and reduce the oven temperature to 200°C (400°F). Remove a third of the glaze and place in a large frying pan over medium-high heat. Cook for 15 minutes or until reduced and thickened.

While the glaze is cooking, turn the ham over and brush with the roasting pan glaze. Cook for a further 15 minutes.

Brush the ham with the reduced and thickened glaze and cook for a further 10 minutes or until golden.

Place the ham on a serving platter and brush with any remaining glaze before carving to serve. SERVES 12–14

bourbon, marmalade and ginger glazed ham

1 x 6–7kg ham leg (see *note*, page 38)
cloves, for decorating
bourbon, marmalade and ginger glaze
1½ cups (510g) store-bought orange marmalade
30g ginger, peeled and thinly sliced
1 clove garlic, crushed
2 cups (480g) firmly packed brown sugar
3 cups (750ml) water
2 tablespoons Dijon mustard
¼ cup (60ml) bourbon

To make the bourbon, marmalade and ginger glaze, place the marmalade, ginger, garlic, sugar, water and mustard in a medium saucepan over medium heat. Bring to a simmer, whisking to combine. Cook for 15 minutes or until slightly reduced. Add the bourbon, whisk to combine and remove from the heat.

Preheat oven to 180°C (350°F).

Lightly grease a large wire rack over a roasting pan. Use a sharp knife to score the skin around the sides and hock of the ham, before using your fingers to gently remove the rind. Trim any excess fat. Wrap the ham hock in non-stick baking paper, then aluminium foil. Score the fat of the ham in a diamond pattern and push 1 clove into the centre of each diamond. Place the ham on the rack and pour the glaze over. Roast, brushing with the glaze every 15 minutes, for 1 hour or until the ham is golden and sticky.

Serve the ham with any remaining glaze. SERVES 12–14

bourbon, marmalade and ginger glazed ham

spiced pomegranate and orange glazed ham

spiced pomegranate and orange glazed ham

1 x 6–7kg ham leg (see *note*, page 38)
4 oranges, peeled, thinly sliced and patted dry
spiced pomegranate and orange glaze
2 sticks cinnamon
4 star-anise
1 cup (250ml) fresh orange juice
1½ cups (360g) firmly packed brown sugar
¼ cup (60ml) pomegranate molasses
¼ cup (90g) honey

Preheat oven to 180°C (350°F).

To make the spiced pomegranate and orange glaze, place the cinnamon, star-anise, juice, sugar, pomegranate molasses and honey in a medium saucepan over medium heat and bring to the boil, stirring to dissolve the sugar. Cook for 4–6 minutes or until syrupy.

Lightly grease a large wire rack over a roasting pan. Use a sharp knife to score the skin around the sides and hock of the ham, before using your fingers to gently remove the rind. Trim any excess fat. Wrap the ham hock in non-stick baking paper, then aluminium foil. Place the ham, top-side down, on the rack and brush with the glaze. Arrange the orange slices over the ham, overlapping slightly. Carefully brush with the glaze and roast the ham for 40 minutes, brushing with glaze halfway. Increase the oven temperature to 200°C (400°F). Brush the ham with the glaze and roast for a further 5 minutes or until golden and caramelised.

Serve the ham with the remaining glaze. SERVES 12–14

apple, maple and miso glazed ham

1 x 6–7kg ham leg (see *note*, page 38)
2 red apples, thinly sliced using a mandoline
cloves, for decorating
apple, maple and miso glaze
1 litre cloudy apple juice
2 cups (480g) firmly packed brown sugar
1 cup (250 ml) pure maple syrup
1 cup (250 ml) apple cider vinegar
2 tablespoons finely grated ginger
¼ cup (55g) white miso paste

To make the apple, maple and miso glaze, place the juice, sugar, maple, vinegar, ginger and miso in a large saucepan over high heat. Cook, stirring, until the sugar is dissolved. Bring to the boil and cook for 20 minutes or until reduced by a quarter and syrupy. Remove from the heat. Strain the glaze into a heatproof jug, discarding any solids.

Preheat oven to 200°C (400°F).

Use a sharp knife to score the skin around the sides and hock of the ham, before using your fingers to gently remove the rind. Trim any excess fat. Wrap the ham hock in non-stick baking paper, then aluminium foil. Pour the glaze into a deep-sided roasting pan. Carefully place the ham, top-side down, into the pan and brush with the glaze. Roast for 40 minutes.

Turn the ham over and arrange the apple slices over the top, overlapping slightly. Stud a clove through the centre of each apple slice to secure it. Roast, brushing with the glaze every 10 minutes, for a further 40 minutes or until golden and sticky.

Brush the remaining glaze over the ham before carving. SERVES 12–14

Apple slices are a *clever way to dress up* the ham *while infusing it with flavour.* Cover the foil on the ham hock with fabric before serving.

apple, maple and miso glazed ham

season the turkey breast

brown both sides

poached turkey breast with lemon and thyme gravy

1 tablespoon extra virgin olive oil

100g unsalted butter

1 x 1.5kg turkey breast fillet, skin on
(see *cook's tips*, page 51)

sea salt and cracked black pepper

4 eschalots (French shallots), peeled and halved

3 cups (750ml) good-quality chicken stock

10 sprigs lemon thyme

1 tablespoon finely shredded lemon rind

1 teaspoon black peppercorns

¼ cup (35g) plain (all-purpose) flour

pour in the stock

strain the poaching liquid

Heat the oil and half the butter in a large heavy-based saucepan over medium heat. Sprinkle the turkey with salt and pepper and add to the pan, skin-side down, with the eschalots. Cook the turkey for 5 minutes each side or until golden. Add the stock, thyme, lemon rind and peppercorns and bring to a simmer. Reduce the heat to low, cover with a tight-fitting lid and poach for 30 minutes or until the turkey is cooked through.

Remove the turkey from the poaching liquid, cover with aluminium foil and set aside to keep warm. Strain the poaching liquid into a heatproof jug, discarding the solids.

Melt the remaining 50g butter in a large saucepan over high heat until bubbling. Add the flour and cook, stirring, for 2–3 minutes or until golden. Gradually pour in the poaching liquid, stirring until smooth. Cook, stirring continuously, for a further 2 minutes or until the gravy has thickened.

Place the turkey on a serving platter. Slice and serve with the gravy (see *cook's tips*, page 51). SERVES 4-6

make a roux for the gravy   add the poaching liquid

poached turkey breast with
lemon and thyme gravy

o Substitute a little of the
chicken stock for white wine
if you wish, and add a couple
of bay leaves to the poaching
liquid for extra flavour.

lemon and thyme gravy

cook's tips

○ It goes without saying that choosing to serve a turkey breast, instead of roasting the entire bird, is an easier option. But it's also a good solution if you're short on time, are having a small simple Christmas, or wish to include turkey as part of your festive banquet menu.

○ This recipe will serve 6–8 if part of a menu. If you wish to serve the turkey as a main with just a couple of sides, it will serve 4–6.

○ By poaching the turkey breast, not only will you end up with tender, succulent meat infused with the delicious flavours it was cooked in, you'll also create a tasty stock to enrich your gravy. It'll mean one less dish crowding the oven, too – the turkey can simmer on the stovetop while a glazed ham, a loin of pork or trays of vegetables are roasting below.

○ It's important to use a good heavy-based saucepan for this recipe, and why not use the same saucepan that the turkey was poached in to make the gravy – easy!

carving turkey

YOU WILL NEED
a large wooden chopping board
a large cook's knife
a large carving fork

step 1

step 3

1. Using a large, sharp knife, cut straight down the side of the turkey to remove the legs, with drumstick and thigh as 1 piece. You may need to apply a little pressure to get through the joint.

3. Cut the leg through the joint to separate the thigh from the drumstick. Slice the breast across the grain into pieces to serve. Repeat with the other side of the turkey.
Tip: Even if you're not serving the whole turkey, it's best to carve it all at once, as meat left on the bone will often continue cooking and dry out. Leftovers will then remain juicy and they'll take up less room in the fridge.

step 2

2. Locate the breastbone, cut down the centre of the turkey and then along the side of the bone away from you to remove the whole breast, with the wing still attached.

ginger-brined roast turkey with pear and potato gratin

ginger-brined roast turkey with pear and potato gratin

1 x 5kg turkey
80g unsalted butter, softened
ginger brine
1 cup (240g) firmly packed brown sugar
1 onion, peeled and quartered
1 head garlic, peeled and halved horizontally
2 cups (600g) rock salt
1 cup (250ml) apple cider vinegar
25g ginger, peeled and thinly sliced
5 litres water
1.25 litres dry ginger ale
pear stuffing
2 tablespoons extra virgin olive oil
1 onion, finely chopped
2 cloves garlic, crushed
2 William (firm green) pears, peeled, cored and chopped
⅓ cup rosemary leaves, chopped
sea salt and cracked black pepper
¼ cup (95g) chopped stem ginger[+]
1 tablespoon Dijon mustard
½ cup (80g) toasted pine nuts
4 cups (280g) sourdough breadcrumbs
1 egg
pear and potato gratin
2.5kg sebago (starchy) potatoes, peeled and thinly sliced
4 William (firm green) pears, peeled, cored and thinly sliced
½ cup (125ml) pure cream

To make the ginger brine, place the sugar, onion, garlic, salt, vinegar, ginger and 1 litre of the water in a large saucepan over high heat. Bring to the boil, stirring to dissolve the salt. Allow to cool slightly. Pour the brining liquid into a large (10-litre-capacity) non-reactive container[++]. Add the dry ginger ale and the remaining water and stir to combine. Using your hands, carefully loosen the skin from the flesh of the turkey breasts. Lower the turkey, breast-side down, into the brine. Cover and refrigerate for 6 hours (but no longer).

To make the pear stuffing, place the oil in a large non-stick frying pan over high heat. Add the onion and garlic and cook, stirring, for 4 minutes. Add the pear, rosemary, salt and pepper and cook for 2 minutes. Transfer to a large bowl and add the ginger, mustard, pine nuts, breadcrumbs and egg. Mix well to combine.

Remove the turkey from the container, discarding the brine, and pat dry with absorbent kitchen paper. Spoon the stuffing into the cavity. Using your hands, spread the butter under the skin. Tie the legs with kitchen string, tuck the wings underneath and set aside.

Preheat oven to 200°C (400°F).

To make the pear and potato gratin, lightly grease a 29cm x 40cm deep-sided roasting pan. Layer the potato and pear in the base of the pan and sprinkle with salt.

Heat the cream in a small saucepan over medium heat for 5 minutes or until hot. Pour the cream over the gratin.

Top the gratin with the turkey. Cover with aluminium foil and roast for 1 hour. Remove the foil, reduce the oven temperature to 180°C (350°F) and roast for a further 1 hour or until the turkey is golden and the juices run clear when tested with a skewer. Cover with aluminium foil and allow to rest for 20 minutes, before serving. SERVES 6–8

+ *Stem ginger is ginger that's been preserved in sugar syrup. It's available from specialty grocers and Asian supermarkets. If unavailable, you can use crystallised ginger instead.*
++ *Non-reactive materials include glass, plastic and stainless steel.*

Brining the turkey first ensures a *succulent bird,* while spreading butter under its skin creates that coveted *golden sheen.* My sweet, herby stuffing and pear-laced gratin seal the deal!

prosecco-brined turkey breast with brussels sprouts and speck

2 x 1.5kg turkey breast fillets, skin on
1 tablespoon extra virgin olive oil
sea salt and cracked black pepper
350g speck or bacon, chopped
500g Brussels sprouts, halved
prosecco brine
¼ cup (75g) rock salt
¼ cup (60g) firmly packed brown sugar
2 sprigs tarragon
2 bunches thyme (about 12 sprigs), plus 1 bunch
   (about 6 sprigs) extra
1 lemon, thinly sliced
1.25 litres water
3 cups (750ml) prosecco
lemon garlic butter
100g unsalted butter, softened
1 clove garlic, crushed
1 teaspoon finely grated lemon rind

To make the prosecco brine, place the salt, sugar, tarragon, thyme, lemon and 2 cups (500ml) of the water in a medium saucepan over high heat. Bring to the boil and cook for 4 minutes, stirring to dissolve the salt. Allow to cool slightly. Pour the brining liquid into a large (5-litre-capacity) non-reactive container+. Add the prosecco and another 2 cups (500ml) of the water. Using your hands, carefully loosen the skin from the flesh of the turkey breasts. Lower the turkey, skin-side down, into the brine. Cover and refrigerate for 2 hours (but no longer).

To make the lemon garlic butter, place the butter, garlic and lemon rind in a small bowl and mix to combine.

Remove the turkey from the container, discarding the brine, and pat dry with absorbent kitchen paper. Using your hands, spread the lemon garlic butter under the skin.

Place the oil in a large heavy-based frying pan over medium heat. Sprinkle the turkey with salt and pepper. Add 1 turkey breast to the pan, skin-side down. Cook for 4 minutes each side or until golden brown. Remove from the pan and repeat with the remaining turkey. Return both turkey breasts to the pan, skin-side up. Add the remaining 1 cup (250ml) of water, cover with a tight-fitting lid and cook for 20 minutes or until golden and cooked through. Remove the turkey from the pan, loosely cover with aluminium foil and reserve the cooking liquid.

Wipe the pan out and return to medium heat. Add the speck and cook, stirring, for 4 minutes or until crispy. Remove and set aside. Increase the heat to high, add the Brussels sprouts and cook, stirring, for 1 minute or until lightly charred. Add the extra thyme and reserved liquid and cook for 2 minutes.

Serve the turkey with the Brussels sprouts and crispy speck. SERVES 4–6
+ *Non-reactive materials include glass, plastic and stainless steel.*

prosecco-brined turkey breast with brussels sprouts and speck

redcurrant-glazed roast turkey with crispy tarragon

redcurrant-glazed roast turkey with crispy tarragon

12 heads single-clove garlic[+], skin on
1 x 4kg turkey, butterflied and halved[++]
sea salt and cracked black pepper
¼ cup (60ml) extra virgin olive oil
2 bunches tarragon (about 12 sprigs)
redcurrant glaze
1 sprig bay leaves (about 6 leaves)
2 sprigs rosemary
1 cup (320g) store-bought redcurrant jelly
2 tablespoons Dijon mustard
1 cup (250ml) red wine
½ cup (125ml) pure maple syrup
2 cups (500ml) good-quality chicken stock

Preheat oven to 180°C (350°F).

To make the redcurrant glaze, place the bay leaves, rosemary, jelly, mustard, wine, maple and stock in a medium saucepan over medium heat and bring to the boil, whisking until combined. Pour the glaze into a large deep-sided roasting pan and add the garlic. Add the turkey, skin-side up, and sprinkle with salt and pepper. Cover with aluminium foil and roast for 1 hour. Remove the foil and roast, brushing every 15 minutes with the pan juices, for a further 45 minutes or until the turkey is sticky and golden and the juices run clear when tested with a skewer. Carefully remove the turkey from the pan, reserving the garlic and any glaze. Loosely cover the turkey with aluminium foil and allow to rest for 20 minutes.

Heat the oil in a medium non-stick frying pan over medium heat. Working in batches, add the tarragon and cook for 30 seconds or until crisp.

Top the turkey with the crispy tarragon, sprinkle with pepper and serve with the reserved garlic and glaze. SERVES 6–8

+ *Single-clove garlic is available from greengrocers. If you can't find it, use large unpeeled garlic cloves.*
++ *Butterflying a turkey allows it to cook faster and more evenly. To butterfly a turkey, position the turkey, breast-side down, on a board so the back is facing up and the drumsticks are facing towards you. Using sharp kitchen scissors or chicken shears, cut closely along both sides of the backbone, remove the bone and discard. Turn the turkey breast-side up, and press down firmly on the breastbone to flatten. To halve, use a sharp knife to cut the turkey down the centre. You can ask your butcher to butterfly the turkey for you.*

Sweet and sticky, with crispy tarragon leaves for extra yum, this turkey is butterflied to save time and to help it cook more evenly. All the juicy flavour *without the fuss.*

lemon thyme-brined turkey

lemon thyme-brined turkey

1 x 5–6kg turkey
2 tablespoons extra virgin olive oil
1 orange, quartered
24 sprigs lemon thyme
4 brown onions, peeled and halved
2 heads garlic, peeled and halved horizontally
1 litre good-quality chicken stock
125g unsalted butter
1 cup (240g) firmly packed brown sugar
lemon thyme brine
1 cup (140g) sea salt flakes
1 cup (240g) firmly packed brown sugar
1 tablespoon fennel seeds, crushed
1 tablespoon lemon thyme leaves
1 tablespoon cracked black pepper

Brine the turkey the day before. To make the lemon thyme brine, place the salt, sugar, fennel seeds, lemon thyme and pepper in a bowl and mix to combine. Place the turkey on a wire rack over a large container or tray and sprinkle evenly with the brine. Refrigerate, uncovered, for 24 hours. Brush off any excess brine mixture.

Preheat oven to 160°C (325°F).

Place the turkey in a large greased baking tray and drizzle with the oil. Fill the cavity of the turkey with the orange and half the lemon thyme sprigs. Arrange the onion, garlic and remaining lemon thyme sprigs around the turkey. Pour 1 cup (250ml) of the chicken stock into the tray and cover tightly with aluminium foil.

Roast the turkey, rotating the tray every hour and adding 1 cup (250ml) of the chicken stock each time, for 2 hours 30 minutes–3 hours.

Place the butter and brown sugar in a small saucepan over medium heat and stir until melted and smooth. Brush the glaze all over the turkey.

Increase the oven temperature to 200°C (400°F) and continue to roast the turkey for 20–30 minutes or until the skin is deeply browned all over. (If the skin is browning too quickly, especially at the breast, cover with foil.)

Transfer the turkey to a large serving platter with the garlic and onion. Pour the pan juices into a small saucepan, add the remaining stock and bring to the boil. Continue to gently boil until the gravy is reduced by half.

Carve the turkey and serve drizzled with the gravy.
SERVES 6-8

rolled turkey with maple and bacon stuffing

1 x 1.8kg turkey breast fillet, skin on
maple and bacon stuffing
50g unsalted butter, chopped
4 rashers bacon, finely chopped
1 brown onion, finely chopped
2 cloves garlic, crushed
500g Granny Smith (green) apples, peeled, cored and grated
1 tablespoon thyme leaves, chopped
3 cups (210g) coarse fresh breadcrumbs
1 tablespoon finely grated orange rind
¼ cup (60ml) pure maple syrup
sea salt and cracked black pepper
orange and maple glaze
100g unsalted butter, chopped
½ cup (125ml) pure maple syrup
½ cup (125ml) fresh orange juice
1 stick cinnamon

To make the maple and bacon stuffing, place the butter in a large non-stick frying pan over high heat. Add the bacon, onion and garlic and cook, stirring, for 4–5 minutes or until lightly browned. Add the apple and thyme and cook for 4–5 minutes or until golden. Transfer to a large bowl and add the breadcrumbs, orange rind, maple, salt and pepper. Mix to combine and allow to cool completely.

To make the orange and maple glaze, place the butter, maple, juice and cinnamon in a small saucepan over high heat and cook, stirring, until the butter is melted. Bring to the boil and cook for 8–10 minutes or until reduced slightly.

Preheat oven to 200°C (400°F).

Lightly grease a wire rack and place over a roasting pan. Place the turkey, skin-side down, on a board. Cut the thickest part of the breast horizontally and open out to make one even fillet. Cover with 2 layers of plastic wrap and, using a meat mallet, flatten to 1.5cm thick. Remove the wrap and arrange the stuffing down one long edge of the fillet. Sprinkle with salt and pepper and roll to enclose. Secure with kitchen string and place the turkey on the rack. Brush with the glaze and roast for 20 minutes. Brush again and roast for 10–20 minutes or until golden and cooked through. Cover with lightly greased aluminium foil and allow to rest for 10 minutes. Place the remaining glaze in a small saucepan over high heat. Bring to the boil and cook for 1–2 minutes or until warmed through.

Slice the turkey and serve with the warm glaze. **SERVES 6-8**

rolled turkey with maple and bacon stuffing

vincotto roasted chicken with herb and sherry stuffing

vincotto roasted chicken
with herb and sherry stuffing

1 x 1.8kg chicken
¼ cup (60ml) vincotto
2 bunches (600g) sweet black seedless grapes,
   cut into small bunches
tarragon butter
¼ cup finely chopped tarragon leaves
100g unsalted butter, softened
sea salt and cracked black pepper
herb and sherry stuffing
50g unsalted butter
2 eschalots (French shallots), finely chopped
2 tablespoons thyme leaves
1 tablespoon finely chopped rosemary leaves
½ cup (125ml) dry sherry
3 cups (210g) fresh sourdough breadcrumbs

To make the tarragon butter, place the tarragon, butter, salt
and pepper in a small bowl and mix until smooth. Set aside.

To make the herb and sherry stuffing, melt the butter
in a large non-stick frying pan over medium heat. Add the
eschalot, thyme, rosemary, salt and pepper and cook,
stirring, for 3–4 minutes, or until soft. Add the sherry
and cook for 1–2 minutes or until syrupy. Remove from
the heat, add the breadcrumbs and mix to combine.

Preheat oven to 180°C (350°F).

Lightly grease a large heavy-based baking dish. Using
your hands, carefully loosen the skin from the flesh of the
chicken breasts and push the tarragon butter underneath.
Fill the cavity of the chicken with the stuffing and tie
the legs with kitchen string to secure. Place the chicken
in the dish. Brush with 1 tablespoon of the vincotto and
sprinkle with salt and pepper. Roast for 40 minutes.
Add the grapes to the dish and drizzle with the remaining
2 tablespoons of vincotto. Roast for a further 30 minutes
or until the chicken is golden and cooked through and the
grapes are soft.

Sprinkle the chicken with pepper to serve. **SERVES 6–8**

bacon-wrapped spatchcocks
with fig and herb stuffing

4 x 500g spatchcocks (baby chickens)
¾ cup (240g) store-bought fruit chutney, plus extra to serve
20 slices streaky bacon
6 x 3cm-thick slices brioche loaf
¼ cup (60ml) extra virgin olive oil
1 bunch sage (about 6 sprigs)
fig and herb stuffing
1 tablespoon extra virgin olive oil
1 onion, finely chopped
2 cloves garlic, crushed
¼ cup (50g) dried figs, chopped
1 tablespoon dried currants
2 tablespoons dried cranberries, chopped
2 tablespoons red wine vinegar
½ cup flat-leaf parsley leaves, finely chopped
¼ cup sage leaves, finely chopped
2 teaspoons Dijon mustard
2½ cups (450g) torn brioche loaf
sea salt and cracked black pepper

Preheat oven to 180°C (350°F).

To make the fig and herb stuffing, place the oil in a large
non-stick frying pan over medium heat. Add the onion,
garlic, figs, currants and cranberries and cook, stirring, for
4 minutes or until softened. Add the vinegar and cook
for 2 minutes. Transfer to a large bowl. Add the parsley,
sage, mustard, torn brioche, salt and pepper and mix well
to combine.

Spoon the stuffing into the cavity of each spatchcock
and tie the legs with kitchen string. Brush 1 tablespoon of
the chutney over each spatchcock. Wrap each spatchcock in
bacon. Place the brioche slices in a large, deep-sided roasting
pan and spread with the remaining chutney. Top with the
spatchcocks and roast for 30 minutes or until golden and
cooked through.

While the spatchcocks are roasting, heat the oil in a
small non-stick frying pan over high heat. Working in
batches, cook the sage for 30 seconds or until crisp.

Sprinkle the spatchcocks with pepper and serve with
the crispy sage and extra chutney. **SERVES 4**

bacon-wrapped spatchcocks with fig and herb stuffing

port and pistachio-stuffed chicken with quince glaze

port and pistachio-stuffed chicken with quince glaze

1 x 1.7kg chicken
2 tablespoons extra virgin olive oil
port and pistachio stuffing
100g unsalted butter
1 brown onion, finely chopped
2 cloves garlic, crushed
⅓ cup (80ml) port
3 cups (210g) fresh sourdough breadcrumbs
1 teaspoon finely grated orange rind
1 tablespoon thyme leaves, finely chopped
½ cup (70g) shelled pistachios, roughly chopped
⅓ cup (50g) dried cherries[+]
sea salt and cracked black pepper
quince glaze
1¼ cups (300g) store-bought quince jelly
1 tablespoon malt vinegar

Preheat oven to 180°C (350°F).

To make the port and pistachio stuffing, melt the butter in a medium non-stick frying pan over medium heat. Add the onion and garlic and cook, stirring, for 6 minutes or until soft. Add the port and cook for a further 2 minutes. Transfer to a large bowl and add the breadcrumbs, orange rind, thyme, pistachios, cherries, salt and pepper. Mix well to combine.

Line a baking tray with non-stick baking paper. Fill the cavity of the chicken with the stuffing. Place on the tray and tie the legs with kitchen string. Rub the skin with oil and sprinkle with salt. Roast for 1 hour or until golden and cooked through.

To make the quince glaze, place the jelly and vinegar in a small saucepan over low heat. Cook, stirring, for 3–4 minutes or until syrupy.

Brush the chicken with the glaze, placing any extra in a jug, to serve. **SERVES 4**

+ You can use dried cranberries in place of the cherries.

spice-rubbed roast duck with cherry sauce

1 x 2.3kg duck
4 cloves
1 teaspoon fennel seeds
½ teaspoon cumin seeds
1 teaspoon ground allspice
1 teaspoon brown sugar
2 teaspoons sea salt flakes
1 small orange, quartered
1½ cups (330g) caster (superfine) sugar
¼ cup (60ml) Campari
2½ cups (375g) frozen pitted cherries
3 sticks cinnamon
4 star-anise
4 strips orange peel
25g ginger, peeled and thinly sliced

Lightly grease a large wire rack over a deep-sided roasting pan. Using a skewer, pierce the skin of the duck all over. Place the duck in a heatproof bowl, cover with boiling water and allow to stand for 30 seconds. Drain, place on the rack and pat dry with absorbent kitchen paper.

Place the cloves, fennel and cumin seeds in a mortar and pound with a pestle until fine. Add the allspice, brown sugar and salt and mix to combine. Rub the spice mixture all over the duck. Place the orange quarters in the cavity and fasten with a metal skewer. Refrigerate, uncovered, for 1 hour or until the skin is dry.

Preheat oven to 180°C (350°F).

Roast the duck for 45 minutes. Remove the pan from the oven and carefully set the duck aside on the rack. Drain any excess fat from the pan juices. Add the caster sugar, Campari, cherries, cinnamon, star-anise, orange peel and ginger to the pan and mix to combine. Return the rack with the duck to sit over the pan and roast for a further 1 hour or until the cherry sauce is sticky and reduced and the duck is golden.

Serve the duck with the cherry sauce. **SERVES 4–6**

score the pork rind

sprinkle with salt

rub the salt in well

spoon the stuffing inside

spread evenly to coat

roll up and tie to secure

roasted pork loin with sour cherry stuffing

1 x 3kg boneless pork loin, trimmed
⅓ cup (40g) sea salt flakes
2 tablespoons extra virgin olive oil
sour cherry stuffing
1 tablespoon extra virgin olive oil
1 small brown onion, finely chopped
2 cloves garlic, crushed
2 tablespoons thyme leaves
3 cups (210g) fresh sourdough breadcrumbs
1 egg
1 tablespoon Dijon mustard
¼ cup (35g) shelled unsalted pistachios, chopped
⅓ cup (90g) sour cherry relish (see *recipe*, page 71),
　plus extra to serve+
sea salt and cracked black pepper

Score the pork rind at 1cm intervals. Sprinkle the rind with 2 tablespoons of the salt and rub in to coat. Refrigerate the pork, uncovered, for 2–3 hours (see *cook's tips*, page 71).

While the pork is resting, make the sour cherry stuffing. Heat the oil in a medium non-stick frying pan over medium heat. Add the onion, garlic and thyme and cook, stirring, for 5–6 minutes or until just golden. Transfer the mixture to a large bowl and add the breadcrumbs, egg, mustard, pistachios, relish, salt and pepper. Mix well to combine and set aside.

Preheat oven to 220°C (425°F).

Lightly grease a wire rack over a roasting pan lined with non-stick baking paper. Brush the salt from the pork and pat with absorbent kitchen paper to remove any excess moisture. Turn the pork, rind-side down, and spread evenly with the stuffing. Roll to enclose and secure with kitchen string. Brush the rind with the oil and rub with the remaining 2 tablespoons of salt, pushing it into the incisions. Place the pork on the rack and roast for 25 minutes. Reduce the oven temperature to 200°C (400°F) and roast for a further 30–40 minutes or until cooked to your liking. Cover with aluminium foil and allow to rest for 15 minutes.

Remove the foil and kitchen string and place the pork on a serving platter. Slice and serve with extra relish. SERVES 6–8
+ *You can use store-bought cranberry sauce instead of the sour cherry relish, if you prefer.*

roasted pork loin with sour cherry stuffing

sour cherry relish

sour cherry relish

1 tablespoon extra virgin olive oil
1 small brown onion, finely chopped
1 tablespoon thyme leaves
500g frozen pitted cherries
1 tablespoon finely grated orange rind
¼ cup (60ml) orange liqueur
⅓ cup (80ml) red wine vinegar
1 cup (220g) caster (superfine) sugar
sea salt and cracked black pepper

Place the oil in a medium saucepan over medium heat.
Add the onion and thyme and cook for 1–2 minutes or
until just golden. Add the cherries, orange rind, liqueur,
vinegar, sugar, salt and pepper and stir to combine. Bring
to the boil and cook for 30–35 minutes or until reduced
and glossy. Allow to cool completely at room temperature.
MAKES 2 CUPS
*Tip: This relish will keep refrigerated in an airtight container
for up to 2 weeks. Bring to room temperature before serving.*

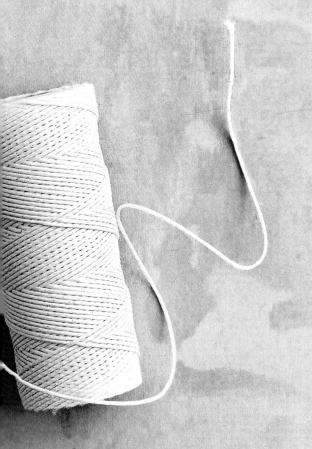

cook's tips

_____

○ Salty, crunchy crackling
is arguably the most
sought-after part of roast
pork. There are a few simple
tricks to making sure it's
extra-crispy every time.
Drying out the rind of the
pork, before roasting, is
important. If time permits,
the day before you roast the
pork, place it, uncovered,
on a wire rack over a tray
in the fridge. Leave it
overnight, then dry it with
absorbent kitchen paper.

_____

○ Scoring the rind exposes
more surface area to heat,
making it crisper, faster.

_____

○ Rubbing the skin with oil
and salt adds loads of crunch
to the crackling.

_____

○ Make sure your oven is
nice and hot. Preheat it to
220°C (425°F) and roast the
pork for 25 minutes before
reducing the temperature
for the remaining time.

_____

○ The sour cherry relish can
be used in a similar way to
cranberry sauce. Its tart,
fruity flavour is perfect
with the pork, but it's also
great with ham or turkey.

score the pork rind   rub with sea salt flakes

drizzle and rub in the oil

crispy pork belly with fennel salt

2 tablespoons sea salt flakes
1 x 2kg piece boneless pork belly, rind scored at 1cm intervals
1 tablespoon vegetable oil
peach, chilli and rosemary chutney, to serve (see *recipe*, below)
fennel salt
2 teaspoons fennel seeds, toasted and crushed
2 tablespoons black sea salt flakes[+]

Preheat oven to 180°C (350°F).
Rub half the salt into the pork rind. Drizzle with the oil and rub to coat. Place the pork, rind-side down, in a roasting pan and roast for 1 hour. Increase the oven temperature to 200°C (400°F). Turn the pork, sprinkle the rind with the remaining salt and roast for a further 1 hour or until the rind is golden and crunchy.
To make the fennel salt, place the fennel and black salt in a small bowl and mix to combine.
Slice the pork and place on a serving platter. Sprinkle with the fennel salt and serve with chutney. **SERVES 8-10** .
+ *Black sea salt flakes are available at specialty stores.*

peach, chilli and rosemary chutney

6 peaches, cut into wedges
1 white onion, finely chopped
2 cloves garlic, crushed
½ teaspoon dried chilli flakes
2 sprigs rosemary
1 cup (250ml) apple cider vinegar
1½ cups (330g) caster (superfine) sugar
1 teaspoon sea salt flakes

Place the peach, onion, garlic, chilli, rosemary, vinegar, sugar and salt in a large saucepan over high heat. Bring to the boil, reduce the heat to medium and cook, stirring occasionally, for 40–45 minutes or until thickened[+].
Remove the rosemary sprigs and pour into sterilised jars[++].
Allow to cool. **MAKES 5 CUPS**
+ *To test whether the chutney is ready, chill a small saucer in the freezer. Place a spoonful of chutney on the cold saucer and run your finger through the middle. If the line remains, it's done.*
++ *To sterilise glass jars, preheat oven to 120°C (250°F). Wash the jars and their (metal) lids in soapy water, rinse and place on an oven tray. Heat for 20 minutes. Allow to cool before filling.*
Tip: This chutney will keep refrigerated for up to 3 weeks.

crispy pork belly with fennel salt
peach, chilli and rosemary chutney

fennel-roasted pork leg with baby figs and pickled onions

malt vinegar and bourbon sticky pork belly

pork with balsamic caramelised cherries

tablespoon sea salt flakes
x 2kg piece boneless pork belly, skin scored at 5cm
  intervals and once down the centre (this will create 8 pieces)
tablespoon vegetable oil
8 eschalots (French shallots), peeled and halved
6 sprigs sage
cups (500ml) good-quality chicken stock
cup (250ml) balsamic vinegar
½ tablespoons juniper berries, lightly crushed
2 cups (300g) frozen pitted cherries

Preheat oven to 200°C (400°F).
Rub the salt into the skin of the pork and drizzle with
the oil.
Place the pork, skin-side down, in a deep-sided roasting
pan and roast for 1 hour. Remove any excess fat from
the pan with a spoon and discard.
Turn the pork, add the eschalot, sage, stock, balsamic,
juniper and cherries and cook for a further 45–50 minutes
or until the skin is golden and crisp and the meat is tender.
Serve the pork with the caramelised cherries and
eschalot, and the pan juices. SERVES 8

malt vinegar and bourbon sticky pork belly

cup (250ml) bourbon whiskey
½ cups (375ml) malt vinegar
2 cups (500ml) water
3 cups (720g) firmly packed dark brown sugar
0 cloves garlic, peeled and bruised
cup (350g) golden syrup
2 sticks cinnamon
4 bay leaves
x 2.5kg piece boneless pork belly, skin scored at 5cm
  intervals (this will create 6–8 pieces)
cracked black pepper, for sprinkling

Preheat oven to 180°C (350°F).
Place the bourbon, 1 cup (250ml) of the vinegar, the
water, sugar, garlic, golden syrup, cinnamon and bay leaves
in a medium saucepan over high heat and bring to the boil.
Cook, stirring occasionally, for 2–3 minutes or until
thickened slightly.

It should fit snugly. Pour the sauce over the pork, cover
tightly with aluminium foil and roast for 3 hours 30 minutes.
Turn the pork, add the remaining ½ cup (125ml) of
vinegar and cover with the foil. Roast for a further
30 minutes or until tender. Remove the pork from the
pan, skim the fat from the surface of the sauce and
discard. Strain the sauce into a heatproof jug.
Slice the pork and top with the sauce. Sprinkle with
pepper to serve. SERVES 6–8

fennel-roasted pork leg with baby figs and pickled onions

1 x 4.5kg pork leg, rind scored at 2cm intervals
1 tablespoon extra virgin olive oil
1 teaspoon caraway seeds
1 teaspoon fennel seeds
⅓ cup (40g) sea salt flakes
2 x 400g jars marinated baby figs in syrup+
2 x 440g jars pickled onions, drained
2 sticks cinnamon
1 cup (250ml) water
store-bought grated horseradish (see *note*, page 19), to serve

Line a large deep-sided roasting pan with non-stick baking
paper. Place the pork, rind-side up, in the pan and rub with
the oil. Wrap the hock with non-stick baking paper, then
aluminium foil. Set aside.
Place the caraway and fennel seeds in a mortar and pound
with a pestle until coarsely ground. Add the salt and mix
to combine. Rub the spice mixture into the pork rind and
allow to stand at room temperature for 30 minutes.
Preheat oven to 220°C (425°F).
Roast the pork for 30 minutes. Reduce the oven
temperature to 180°C (350°F) and roast for a further
1 hour 30 minutes.
Carefully remove the pork from the pan. Discard the
pan juices and paper. Add the figs and their syrup, the
pickled onions, cinnamon and water. Mix to combine and
place the pork on top. Increase the oven temperature to
220°C (425°F). Roast for 30 minutes or until the rind is
crisp and the pork is tender.
Serve the pork with the figs, pickled onions and
horseradish. SERVES 8–10
+ *Marinated baby figs are available from delicatessens*

pork with balsamic caramelised cherries

remove from the freezer   halve the lobster

prep the butter mixture   spread it over the flesh

grilled lobster with taramasalata butter

1kg rock salt
4 x 600g green (raw) lobsters, cleaned and halved
  (see *cook's tip*, below)
taramasalata butter
250g unsalted butter, chopped and softened
1 cup (260g) store-bought taramasalata
sea salt and cracked black pepper

To make the taramasalata butter, place the butter,
taramasalata, salt and pepper in a medium bowl. Mix to
combine and set aside.

Preheat oven grill (broiler) to high heat. Divide the rock
salt between 2 large oven trays and spread evenly. Place
the lobster halves, shell-side down, on the salt and spread
the flesh with half the butter mixture. Cook the lobster, in
batches, for 6–8 minutes or until the butter is golden and the
lobster is just cooked. Top with the remaining taramasalata
butter and sprinkle with pepper to serve. **SERVES 8**
*Tip: You can make the taramasalata butter up to 2–3 days
in advance and keep it refrigerated.*

cook's tip

∘ To prepare live lobsters, place them in a
clean tea towel and wrap to enclose. Freeze
for 1 hour to sedate them. Remove and place
1 lobster, shell-side up, on a large chopping
board. Using a large sharp knife, halve the
head section, pressing the knife firmly
from the neck down towards the eyes. Rotate
the board and halve the body section, now
cutting down towards the tail. Clean the
insides, using a spoon to scrape them out.
Pat the flesh dry with absorbent kitchen
paper. Repeat with the remaining lobsters.

grilled lobster with taramasalata butter

rosemary salt baked whole snapper

rosemary salt baked whole snapper

2 cups rosemary leaves
6 cloves garlic
1kg rock salt
2 eggwhites
8 long thick sprigs rosemary, extra
1 x 1.2kg whole snapper, cleaned
1 lemon, sliced

Preheat oven to 220°C (425°F).

Place the rosemary leaves, garlic and ⅓ cup (100g) of the salt in a food processor and process until finely chopped. Transfer to a large bowl and add the remaining 3 cups (900g) of salt. Add the eggwhites and mix to combine.

Place half the salt mixture in the base of a large baking dish. Top with the extra rosemary sprigs and the snapper. Place the lemon in the cavity of the fish. Pour the remaining salt mixture onto the fish and gently press to seal. Roast for 25 minutes or until cooked to your liking.

Allow to cool slightly before carefully removing the salt crust to serve. SERVES 4

Tips: Baking a whole fish in a salt crust not only looks impressive, it keeps moisture in and intensifies flavour. Brush away any extra salt, using a pastry brush, before serving.

portuguese-style barbecued seafood platter

1½ tablespoons smoked paprika
3 teaspoons sweet paprika
1½ teaspoons dried chilli flakes
3 cloves garlic, crushed
1 tablespoon finely grated lemon rind
¾ cup (180ml) extra virgin olive oil
¼ cup (60ml) red wine vinegar
2 x 375g raw blue swimmer crabs
4 scallops on the half shell
6 green (raw) king prawns (shrimp), shells intact
  and halved lengthways
4 sardines, filleted
6 small squid tubes, cleaned
500g mussels, cleaned
sea salt and cracked black pepper
lemon wedges and store-bought aioli (optional), to serve

Preheat a large chargrill pan or barbecue over high heat.

Place the smoked and sweet paprika, the chilli, garlic, lemon rind, oil and vinegar in a small bowl and mix to combine. Reserve and set aside ¼ cup (60ml) of the dressing.

Place the crabs, scallops, prawns, sardines, squid and mussels in a large roasting pan. Drizzle with the paprika dressing and toss to coat.

Add the crabs to the grill and cook, covered[+], for 5 minutes each side. Set aside and keep warm. Add the scallops, shell-side down, and cook, covered, for 3 minutes. Set aside and keep warm. Add the prawns, sardines and squid and cook for 1–2 minutes each side or until charred and just cooked. Set aside and keep warm. Add the mussels and cook, covered, for 1–2 minutes or until opened.

Place the seafood onto a large serving platter. Sprinkle with salt and pepper and drizzle with the reserved dressing. Serve with lemon wedges and aioli, if you like. SERVES 2

+ If using a barbecue, close the lid to cover. If using a chargrill pan, cover with a tight-fitting lid or a large metal bowl.

portuguese-style barbecued seafood platter

There's a new contender for my *favourite festive main*.
With its *cheesy egg filling*, golden base and tangle of crispy leeks
on top, this vegetarian pie is *one botanical beauty!*

leek and gruyère pie

leek and gruyère pie

2 tablespoons extra virgin olive oil
1kg leeks (about 5 leeks), trimmed and thinly sliced
1 tablespoon lemon thyme leaves
2 tablespoons chopped dill leaves
1 tablespoon finely grated lemon rind
2 cups (500ml) pure cream
250g cream cheese, chopped and softened
4 eggs, plus 4 egg yolks extra
150g gruyère, grated
sea salt and cracked black pepper
micro (baby) shiso leaves (see *note*, page 19) (optional),
    to serve
hot water pastry
125g unsalted butter, chopped
1 teaspoon sea salt flakes
¾ cup (180ml) water
1 cup (150g) wholemeal (whole-wheat) plain
    (all-purpose) flour
1½ cups (225g) plain (all-purpose) flour
sage sprigs and leaves, to decorate
fried leeks
100g leeks (about ½ leek), trimmed and sliced into thin strips
vegetable oil, for frying

Preheat oven to 200°C (400°F).

Invert the base of a 24cm round springform tin. Grease the tin and line the base with non-stick baking paper.

To make the hot water pastry, place the butter, salt and water in a medium saucepan over high heat and bring to the boil. Remove from the heat and stir in the flours until a smooth dough forms. Turn out onto a lightly floured surface and knead until smooth. Roll out the pastry between 2 sheets of non-stick baking paper to 3mm-thick. Remove the top sheet of baking paper and discard.

Press the sage leaves and sprigs around the inside of the prepared tin. Using the remaining baking paper to help you, carefully line the tin with the pastry, trimming any excess. Top the baking paper with weights or rice to fill. Blind-bake for 15 minutes. Remove the paper and weights and set aside.

Heat a large frying pan over medium heat. Add the oil, leek, lemon thyme, dill and lemon rind. Cover with a tight-fitting lid and cook for 5 minutes or until softened. Remove the lid and cook, stirring occasionally, for 15–20 minutes or until the leek is golden and caramelised. Allow to cool slightly.

Place the cream, cream cheese, eggs and extra yolks, gruyère, salt and pepper in a large bowl. Whisk to combine. Add the leek mixture and stir through.

Reduce the oven temperature to 180°C (350°F). Pour the leek filling into the tart case and bake for 40–45 minutes or until set and golden. Allow to rest for 10 minutes.

Meanwhile, to make the fried leeks, heat 2cm of vegetable oil in a non-stick frying pan over medium-high heat. Fry the leek, in batches, for 3–5 minutes or until crispy. Remove and drain on absorbent kitchen paper.

Carefully remove the pie from the tin and transfer to a serving plate. Arrange the fried leeks and shiso leaves on top and serve. SERVES 8

sides

Everyone knows it's all about the rainbow of sides on the Christmas table. No longer the back-up dancers, these veg-forward plates are the unsung heroes of the festive season, ready to deliver a fresh hit of deliciousness.

herb and garlic sourdough crouton salad

herb and garlic sourdough crouton salad

1½ cups flat-leaf parsley leaves
1½ cups mint leaves
1 cup basil leaves, roughly torn
4 large oxheart tomatoes, thickly sliced
250g buffalo mozzarella, drained and torn
herb and garlic croutons
350g sourdough bread, roughly torn into pieces
¼ cup (60ml) extra virgin olive oil
2 cloves garlic, crushed
¼ cup oregano leaves
1 leek, thinly sliced
sea salt and cracked black pepper
honey mustard dressing
¼ cup (60ml) red wine vinegar
¼ cup (60ml) extra virgin olive oil
1 tablespoon Dijon mustard
1 tablespoon honey

Preheat oven to 180°C (350°F). Line 2 baking trays with non-stick baking paper.

To make the herb and garlic croutons, place the sourdough, oil, garlic, oregano, leek, salt and pepper in a large bowl and toss to combine. Divide between the prepared trays and bake, swapping the trays halfway through, for 20 minutes or until the croutons are crisp and golden. Allow to cool.

Meanwhile, to make the honey mustard dressing, combine the vinegar, oil, mustard and honey in a bowl.

Place the parsley, mint, basil, tomato and croutons on a large platter. Drizzle with the honey mustard dressing and gently toss to combine. Top with the mozzarella, sprinkle with salt and pepper and serve with the remaining dressing on the side. SERVES 8

blanched bean and prosciutto bundles

800g green beans, trimmed
8 slices prosciutto
micro (baby) herbs (optional) (see *note*, page 19),
    to serve
almond brown butter dressing
60g unsalted butter
¼ cup (35g) slivered almonds
2 tablespoons extra virgin olive oil
2 tablespoons white balsamic or white wine vinegar
2 teaspoons wholegrain mustard
sea salt and cracked black pepper

Cook the beans in a large saucepan of boiling water for 1–2 minutes or until just tender. Drain, refresh under cold running water, drain again and divide into 8 even bundles.

Wrap a slice of prosciutto around a bean bundle, scrunching the prosciutto together to secure. Repeat with the remaining prosciutto and bean bundles.

To make the almond brown butter dressing, melt the butter in a frying pan over high heat until dark brown. Add the almonds and oil. Cook for 2 minutes or until the almonds are toasted. Remove from the heat and stir in the vinegar, mustard, salt and pepper.

Place the bean bundles on a large serving platter. Drizzle the warm dressing over them, scatter with the herbs and serve. SERVES 8

This is *an upscaled version* of that classic Italian bread salad. *Golden herb and garlic croutons* add delicious flavour and crunch!

blanched bean and prosciutto bundles

Italian potato salad

Italian potato salad

1.5kg baby (new) potatoes
1 red onion, finely sliced
1 tablespoon finely grated lemon rind
½ cup (125ml) lemon juice
⅓ cup (80ml) extra virgin olive oil
4 long red chillies, deseeded and finely shredded
⅓ cup (60g) salted baby capers, rinsed
4 cloves garlic, peeled and thinly sliced
⅓ cup flat-leaf parsley leaves, roughly torn
¼ cup fresh dill leaves
100g rocket (arugula), finely chopped
sea salt and cracked black pepper

Place the potatoes in a large saucepan of salted cold water over high heat. Bring to the boil and cook for 18–20 minutes or until tender. Drain and allow to cool. Slice the potatoes into halves or if they're larger, into thirds.

Meanwhile, place the red onion, lemon rind and juice in a glass or non-reactive bowl and set aside to pickle.

Heat the oil in a medium frying pan over medium heat. Add the chilli and capers and cook for 6 minutes or until they start to crisp up. Add the garlic and cook for 3 minutes or until golden.

Place the potatoes, parsley, dill, rocket, pickled onion, salt and pepper in a large serving dish. Add the chilli mixture and the pan juices and drizzle with the onion pickling liquid. Gently toss to combine and serve. SERVES 6-8

pickled beetroot, radicchio and goat's cheese salad

2 tablespoons extra virgin olive oil
3 heads radicchio, trimmed and leaves separated
200g ash-dusted goat's cheese[+], sliced
pickled beetroot
½ cup (125ml) water
1 cup (250ml) apple cider vinegar
⅓ cup (120g) honey
¼ cup sage leaves
sea salt and ground black pepper
3 beetroots, peeled and thinly sliced using a mandoline
4 baby target beetroots[++], scrubbed and thinly sliced using a mandoline
honey walnut clusters
1 cup (100g) walnuts
2 tablespoons honey
1 teaspoon sea salt flakes

To make the pickled beetroot, combine the water, vinegar, honey, sage, salt and pepper in a glass jug. Place the beetroot and target beetroot into 2 separate glass bowls. Add two-thirds of the pickling liquid to the beetroot and the remaining one-third to the target beetroot. Refrigerate both for 2 hours or overnight to pickle.

To make the honey walnut clusters, place the walnuts, honey and salt in a medium non-stick frying pan over medium heat. Cook, stirring, for 3–4 minutes or until golden. Spoon onto a sheet of non-stick baking paper and cool for 10 minutes before breaking into clusters.

When ready to serve, drain both beetroots, reserving ⅓ cup (80ml) of the pickling liquid. Combine the reserved pickling liquid with the oil to make a dressing.

Arrange the radicchio leaves on a serving platter. Top with the pickled beetroot and goat's cheese slices. Scatter the walnut clusters over the top and drizzle with the dressing. Serve immediately. SERVES 8

+ *Ash-dusted goat's cheese is available at select supermarkets and delicatessens. If you can't find it, use regular goat's cheese.*
++ *Baby target beetroots are available at select greengrocers.*

Introducing your *new favourite potato salad*!
The combination of *crunch, cream and zing* is irresistible.

pickled beetroot, radicchio and goat's cheese salad

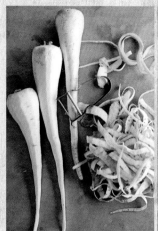

peel the parsnips

sprinkle them with sugar

toss to combine

top with the thyme sprigs

pour in the champagne

thyme and champagne roasted parsnips

2kg parsnips, peeled, quartered and cut into 8cm lengths
½ cup (120g) firmly packed brown sugar
16 sprigs lemon thyme, plus extra to serve
2 cups (500ml) Champagne or sparkling wine
sea salt and cracked black pepper

Preheat oven to 220°C (425°F).
　Divide the parsnip between 2 large roasting pans.
Sprinkle with the sugar and toss to combine. Divide the
thyme and Champagne between the pans, toss to coat
and sprinkle with salt and pepper. Roast, turning halfway,
for 30–35 minutes or until the parsnip is golden
and caramelised.
　Transfer the parsnip to a serving plate, top with extra
thyme and sprinkle with salt and pepper to serve. SERVES 6–8

thyme and champagne roasted parsnips

broccoli with lemon butter and thyme breadcrumbs

broccoli with lemon butter and thyme breadcrumbs

1.5kg broccoli, cut into florets
100g unsalted butter, chopped
1 tablespoon finely shredded lemon rind
1 tablespoon lemon juice
¼ cup (60ml) dry white wine
sea salt and cracked black pepper
½ cup (35g) fresh sourdough breadcrumbs
¼ cup lemon thyme leaves
1 tablespoon extra virgin olive oil

Preheat oven to 200°C (400°F).

Place the broccoli in a large heatproof bowl and cover with boiling water. Allow to stand for 2 minutes, drain well and place in a large roasting pan.

Place the butter, lemon rind, lemon juice and wine in a small saucepan over medium heat and stir until the butter is melted. Pour the sauce over the broccoli and sprinkle with salt and pepper.

Place the breadcrumbs, thyme and oil in a medium bowl and mix to combine. Sprinkle the breadcrumb mixture over the broccoli and roast for 20 minutes or until golden and the broccoli is tender. SERVES 6

pancetta and herb stuffing apples

1 tablespoon extra virgin olive oil
1 onion, finely chopped
2 cloves garlic, thinly sliced
sea salt and cracked black pepper
6 slices pancetta, chopped
2 cups (140g) fresh sourdough breadcrumbs
¼ cup (35g) dried cranberries
1 cup flat-leaf parsley leaves, chopped
¼ cup marjoram leaves
1 egg, lightly whisked
2 tablespoons sherry vinegar
12 x Royal Gala (red) apples

Preheat oven to 180°C (350°F).

Place the oil in a large non-stick frying pan over high heat. Add the onion, garlic, salt and pepper and cook, stirring, for 4–5 minutes or until golden. Transfer to a large bowl. Add the pancetta, breadcrumbs, cranberries, parsley, marjoram, egg and vinegar and mix to combine.

Line a large baking tray with non-stick baking paper. Slice the tops from the apples and set aside. Using a teaspoon, scoop out the cores and discard, leaving the bases of the apples intact. Fill the cavities of the apples with the breadcrumb mixture and place on the tray. Return the tops to the apples and bake for 25–35 minutes or until golden brown and softened.

Allow the apples to cool slightly before serving. MAKES 12

Drenched in a *zesty, lemony sauce,* then blanketed
in a crunchy, *herby sourdough crumb* – this isn't your
average tray of roasted broccoli.

pancetta and herb stuffing apples

honey and almond hasselback pumpkin

Basted with a *delicious herb and garlic butter* as it slowly roasts in the oven, this golden whole head of cauliflower makes a *stunning yet simple side* when it hits the table.

honey and almond hasselback pumpkin

1 x 1.8kg butternut pumpkin (squash), halved lengthways,
    peeled and seeds removed
1 tablespoon extra virgin olive oil
½ cup (180g) honey
2 tablespoons malt vinegar
14 bay leaves
½ cup (80g) almonds, toasted and chopped
sea salt and cracked black pepper

Preheat oven to 220°C (425°F).
    Line a large baking tray with non-stick baking paper.
Place one pumpkin half, cut-side down, on a chopping board.
Place a chopstick, lengthways, on each side of the pumpkin+.
Using a very sharp knife, carefully slice through the pumpkin
to the chopsticks at 5mm intervals. Repeat with the
remaining pumpkin half.
    Place the pumpkin on the tray, cut-side down, and drizzle
with the oil. Cover tightly with aluminium foil and roast
for 30 minutes. Uncover and roast the pumpkin for a
further 25–30 minutes or until golden.
    Place the honey, vinegar and bay leaves in a small
saucepan over high heat. Bring to the boil and cook for
4–5 minutes or until slightly reduced. Remove the bay
leaves and reserve. Spoon half the honey glaze over the
pumpkin and roast for a further 5–10 minutes or until
tender and golden.
    Sprinkle with the almonds, salt and pepper and drizzle
with the remaining honey glaze. Insert the bay leaves into
the incisions to serve. **SERVES 6**
+ *The chopsticks are to help you make deep incisions in the
pumpkin halves, while keeping them intact.*

whole roasted cauliflower
in white wine and garlic butter

1.5kg cauliflower, trimmed with leaves intact
2 cups (500ml) dry white wine
1 cup (250ml) good-quality vegetable or chicken stock
100g unsalted butter, chopped
2 tablespoons Dijon mustard
1 bunch thyme (about 6 sprigs)
8 cloves garlic, skin on
4 strips lemon rind
sea salt and cracked black pepper

Preheat oven to 220°C (425°F).
    Place the cauliflower, wine, stock, butter, mustard,
thyme, garlic, lemon rind, salt and pepper in a deep-sided
roasting pan. Cover tightly with aluminium foil and roast,
basting with the pan juices every 30 minutes, for
1 hour 30 minutes or until tender.
    Uncover, baste with the pan juices and roast for a
further 15 minutes or until golden brown to serve. **SERVES 6**

whole roasted cauliflower in white wine and garlic butter

potato and herb bread wreath

1kg rock salt
1.5kg sebago (starchy) potatoes
1½ cups (375ml) milk
75g unsalted butter, chopped
1½ tablespoons caster (superfine) sugar
3 teaspoons dry yeast
4½ cups (675g) plain (all-purpose) flour
½ teaspoon sea salt flakes
3 eggs
3 cups flat-leaf parsley leaves, finely chopped
¼ cup rosemary leaves, finely chopped
¼ cup thyme leaves
⅓ cup (80ml) extra virgin olive oil

Preheat oven to 220°C (425°F).

Place the rock salt on a baking tray and top with the potatoes. Prick the potatoes all over with a metal skewer and roast for 1 hour or until soft. Allow to cool slightly. Cut the potatoes in half and scoop the flesh into a medium bowl, discarding the skins. Set aside.

While the potato is cooling, place half the milk in a small saucepan over high heat and bring to just below the boil. Remove from the heat, add the butter and sugar and stir until the butter is melted. Add the yeast and the remaining milk and stir to combine. Set aside in a warm place for 5 minutes or until the surface is foamy.

Place the flour, salt, eggs and the yeast mixture in the bowl of an electric mixer fitted with a dough hook and beat for 5 minutes or until the dough is smooth and elastic. Place the dough in a lightly oiled bowl, cover and set aside in a warm place for 30 minutes or until doubled in size.

Sprinkle the dough with the potato and gently knead to combine. Divide the dough into roughly 34 x 1-tablespoon portions and roll into balls.

Line a 24cm round cake tin with non-stick baking paper, allowing 3cm of the paper to extend above the edge. Lightly grease an 8cm-tall x 8cm-wide ovenproof ramekin[+] and position it in the centre of the tin. Place the parsley, rosemary, thyme and oil in a small bowl and mix to combine. Roll the dough balls in the herb mixture and place in the tin. Cover and set aside in a warm place for 30 minutes or until risen.

Preheat oven to 180°C (350°F).

Bake the bread for 25 minutes or until golden brown and cooked through. While still warm, remove the ramekin and allow the bread to cool in the tin for 5 minutes, before turning out and serving. SERVES 8-10

+ *It's important the ramekin is at least 8cm tall, as the dough will continue to rise as it bakes.*

Tips: A sprig or two of fresh bay leaves or rosemary, pushed into the baked bread, makes a lovely addition to the wreath. Place it in the centre of the table for easy sharing and it will double as a festive centrepiece.

potato and herb bread wreath

potato gratin

potato gratin

400g Désireé potatoes[+], thinly sliced
⅓ cup (40g) grated gruyère
⅓ cup (80g) sour cream
1 tablespoon chopped chives
sea salt and cracked black pepper

Preheat oven to 180°C (350°F). Cut 4 x 30cm x 40cm sheets of non-stick baking paper.

Place the potato slices down the centre of each sheet, overlapping them slightly. Combine the gruyère, sour cream, chives, salt and pepper in a bowl. Spoon the gruyère mixture over each of the potato parcels, spreading it over the potatoes. Wrap the paper over the potatoes and fold the ends to enclose the parcels. Place on a baking tray and bake for 45 minutes or until cooked through. **SERVES 4**

+ *If you can't find Désireé potatoes, use any other roasting potatoes instead.*

chestnut, bacon and sage stuffing rolls

50g unsalted butter
2 small brown onions, finely chopped
2 cloves garlic, crushed
100g rindless bacon, finely chopped
⅓ cup (80ml) dry sherry, plus 1 tablespoon extra
8 soft fresh dates (160g), pitted and chopped
1 x 240g can cooked chestnuts[+], chopped
¼ cup (35g) slivered almonds, toasted and chopped
3 cups (210g) fresh breadcrumbs
¼ cup finely chopped sage
¼ cup finely chopped flat-leaf parsley leaves
1 teaspoon finely grated lemon rind
2 eggs, lightly whisked
1 teaspoon sea salt flakes
1 teaspoon cracked black pepper
24 thin slices streaky bacon[++]
2 tablespoons honey

Preheat oven to 180°C (350°F).

Melt the butter in a large non-stick frying pan over medium heat. Add the onion, garlic and bacon and cook, stirring, for 5–6 minutes or until soft. Add the sherry and dates and cook, stirring, for 1 minute. Transfer to a large bowl and add the chestnuts, almonds, breadcrumbs, sage, parsley, lemon rind, egg, salt and pepper. Mix to combine and set aside.

Cut 2 large pieces of aluminium foil and 2 large pieces of non-stick baking paper. Lay 1 piece of foil on a flat surface and top with 1 sheet of baking paper. Arrange 12 of the bacon slices, overlapping slightly, on the paper. Place half the stuffing along one edge of the bacon and shape into a log. Using the foil and paper to help you, roll the bacon to enclose the stuffing, wrapping to secure. Repeat with the remaining foil, baking paper, bacon and stuffing. Place the rolls on a baking tray and roast for 20 minutes.

Place the extra sherry and honey in a small bowl and mix to combine. Remove the rolls from the foil and paper and return to the tray. Brush with the honey glaze and roast for a further 20 minutes or until crisp. Slice to serve. **SERVES 8-10**

+ *Buy canned chestnuts from grocers and specialty food shops.*
++ *Ask your butcher to thinly slice streaky bacon for you, or use flat pancetta slices.*
Tip: These rolls can be assembled 2 days ahead and refrigerated. If you want to serve them alongside pork or turkey, simply add them to the same oven in the last 40 minutes of roasting time.

chestnut, bacon and sage stuffing rolls

crispy leaf potatoes with oregano salt

crispy leaf potatoes with oregano salt

5.5kg large sebago (starchy) potatoes, peeled
1¼ cups (310g) duck fat+, melted
1 tablespoon sea salt flakes
1 teaspoon cracked black pepper
oregano salt
¼ cup oregano leaves
2 tablespoons sea salt flakes

Preheat oven to 200°C (400°F).
   Trim the rounded edges of each potato to make large
rectangles and thinly slice on a mandoline. Place in a
large bowl, add the duck fat, salt and pepper and toss
to combine.
   Working along the short edge of a 24cm x 37cm roasting
pan, arrange the potato upright from right to left to fill
the pan. Roast for 1 hour 15 minutes or until golden
and crisp.
   To make the oregano salt, place the oregano and half
the salt in a small food processor and process until finely
chopped. Transfer to a small bowl, add the remaining salt
and mix to combine.
   Sprinkle the potatoes with oregano salt to serve. SERVES 8–10
+ *You can buy duck fat in jars or tins at delicatessens, specialty
grocers and at most supermarkets.*

glazed root vegetable tarte tatin

2 medium carrots (240g), peeled
2 medium parsnips (500g), peeled
2 small sweet potatoes (kumara) (350g), peeled
2 turnips (450g), peeled
¼ cup (60ml) extra virgin olive oil
sea salt and cracked black pepper
⅓ cup (80ml) water
1 cup (220g) caster (superfine) sugar
1 tablespoon red wine vinegar
100g stracchino+, sliced
4 sheets store-bought ready-rolled butter puff pastry, thawed
1 bunch lemon thyme (about 6 sprigs), to serve

Preheat oven to 220°C (425°F).
   Slice the carrots, parsnips, sweet potatoes and turnips
into 1cm-thick rounds. Divide between 2 baking trays,
drizzle with the oil and sprinkle with salt and pepper.
Toss to combine and roast, turning halfway, for 30 minutes
or until golden and tender.
   While the vegetables are roasting, place the water and
sugar in a medium saucepan over medium heat and cook,
stirring, until the sugar is dissolved. Increase the heat to high
and cook, without stirring, for 6–8 minutes or until light
caramel in colour. Remove from the heat and carefully
add the vinegar, stirring to combine. Working quickly, pour
the caramel evenly onto a 24cm x 37cm roasting pan++.
Arrange the vegetables on top of the caramel, overlapping
if necessary, and top with the cheese. Place the 4 sheets
of pastry over the top of the vegetables (pastry will overlap)
allowing 2cm to overhang around the edge of the pan.
Gently press the overlapping pastry to seal and tuck in
the overhanging edges.
   Reduce the oven temperature to 200°C (400°F). Place
the tart on a baking tray to catch any spills and bake for
20 minutes. Reduce the oven temperature to 180°C (350°F)
and bake for a further 20 minutes or until the pastry is
puffed and golden. Allow to stand in the pan for 5 minutes
before inverting onto a board.
   Top with the thyme and cut into squares to serve. SERVES 8–10
+ *Stracchino is a young Italian cow's milk cheese. Find it in
delicatessens and cheese stores. Use taleggio if unavailable.*
++ *Use a metal spoon to spread the caramel over the base
of the pan. Don't worry if it doesn't spread all the way to
the corners – it will spread as it bakes.*

glazed root vegetable tarte tatin

cauliflower, caramelised onion and fontina gratin

cauliflower, caramelised onion and fontina gratin

1.5kg cauliflower, trimmed and cut into florets
½ cup (140g) store-bought caramelised onion relish
1⅔ cups (410ml) pure cream
2½ cups (250g) grated fontina or gruyère
sea salt and cracked black pepper
2 tablespoons extra virgin olive oil
12 small sage leaves
finely grated parmesan, to serve

Preheat oven to 180°C (350°F). Line 2 x 30cm round baking dishes with non-stick baking paper.

Cut the cauliflower florets into 1cm-thick slices and arrange them in the dishes, placing 1-teaspoon portions of caramelised onion relish between the overlapping slices. Drizzle with the cream and top with the fontina, salt and pepper. Bake for 30 minutes or until the cauliflower is just tender and the cheese is golden.

While the gratin is baking, heat the oil in a small non-stick frying pan over medium heat. Cook the sage leaves, in batches, for 30 seconds or until crisp.

Top the gratin with the crispy sage leaves and parmesan to serve. SERVES 8–10

roasted pear and rosemary brioche toasts

1 cup (240g) firmly packed brown sugar
¼ cup (60ml) apple cider vinegar
50g unsalted butter, melted
7 small corella (rosy pink) pears, quartered
1 x 400g brioche loaf
2 tablespoons rosemary leaves
1 teaspoon cracked black pepper

Preheat oven to 220°C (425°F). Line a deep-sided roasting pan with non-stick baking paper.

Place the sugar, vinegar and butter in a large bowl and mix to combine. Reserve and set aside ¼ cup (60ml) of the mixture. Add the pears to the bowl with the sugar mixture and toss to coat. Transfer to the pan and roast, turning halfway, for 15 minutes or until just golden.

Line a 24cm x 37cm baking tray with non-stick baking paper. Slice the brioche loaf into 13 x 2cm-thick slices. Trim the crusts and cut each slice in half. Arrange the brioche to fit snugly on the tray. Top each rectangle with a wedge of roasted pear and pour over any pan juices. Brush each pear with the reserved sugar mixture and sprinkle with the rosemary. Bake for 15 minutes or until the brioche is toasted and the pears are golden.

Brush the pears with any remaining sugar mixture and sprinkle with the pepper to serve. SERVES 8–10
Tips: You can roast the pears 1 day in advance and keep them refrigerated in their cooking juices. Assemble the toasts the next day and bake as instructed. These toasts are perfect served alongside ham and roasted pork.

roasted pear and rosemary brioche toasts

parsnip, sweet potato and thyme yorkshire puddings

Sweet maple-drizzled baby carrots wrapped in a *crispy layer of yum* – this side is the best of the salty and sweet worlds.

parsnip, sweet potato and thyme yorkshire puddings

1 cup (150g) plain (all-purpose) flour
4 eggs
2 teaspoons sea salt flakes
1 teaspoon cracked black pepper
1⅓ cups (330ml) milk
2 teaspoons thyme leaves
½ cup (60g) shaved parsnip⁺
1 cup (120g) shaved sweet potato (kumara)⁺
⅓ cup (80g) ghee (clarified butter), melted

Preheat oven to 220°C (425°F).

Place the flour, eggs, salt, pepper, milk and thyme in a blender and blend until smooth. Allow to stand for 20 minutes. Place the parsnip and sweet potato in a small bowl and toss to combine.

Divide the ghee between 12 x ½-cup-capacity (125ml) muffin tins. Heat in the oven for 12–15 minutes or until the ghee is just smoking. Remove from the oven and, working quickly, pour ¼-cup (60ml) portions of the batter into each tin. Top with the shaved vegetables. Bake for 20–25 minutes or until puffed and golden. Allow to cool in the tins for 5 minutes before turning out to serve. MAKES 12

+ You'll need to buy 1 parsnip and 1 sweet potato for this recipe. Use a vegetable peeler or a mandoline to shave the required amount.

prosciutto-wrapped baby carrots

1kg mixed heirloom baby carrots, trimmed and peeled
8 slices prosciutto, cut into 8cm-long strips
4 bay leaves
8 strips orange rind
2 tablespoons extra virgin olive oil
2 tablespoons pure maple syrup
sea salt and cracked black pepper

Preheat oven to 180°C (350°F). Lightly grease 2 large baking dishes.

Wrap each carrot in a strip of prosciutto. Divide the wrapped carrots, the bay leaves and orange rind between the dishes. Drizzle with the oil and maple syrup and sprinkle with salt and pepper. Roast for 15–18 minutes or until the prosciutto is golden brown and the carrots are tender.

Sprinkle the carrots with extra pepper to serve. SERVES 6-8

prosciutto-wrapped baby carrots

caramelised onion and potato stacks

2 tablespoons extra virgin olive oil
4 brown onions, trimmed and sliced into 16 thick rounds
500g sebago (starchy) potatoes, peeled and thinly sliced
⅔ cup (160ml) good-quality chicken stock
80g unsalted butter, melted
8 sprigs thyme
sea salt and cracked black pepper

Preheat oven to 180°C (350°F). Line 8 x ½-cup capacity
(125ml) muffin tins with non-stick baking paper.

Heat the oil in a large non-stick frying pan over medium
heat. Add the onion slices and cook in batches, turning,
for 3 minutes or until golden.

Place 1 onion slice in the base of each tin. Divide the potato
slices between the tins and top with the remaining onion.

Divide the stock and butter between the tins and top
each with a thyme sprig. Cover with aluminium foil and
roast for 30 minutes. Uncover and roast for a further
30 minutes or until cooked through and golden.

Remove the stacks from the tins and sprinkle with salt
and pepper to serve. MAKES 8

asparagus and feta salad

⅓ cup (80ml) lemon-flavoured extra virgin olive oil
2 tablespoons white balsamic or white wine vinegar
1 tablespoon finely chopped dill leaves
1 tablespoon finely chopped tarragon leaves
1 tablespoon finely chopped chives
1 clove garlic, crushed
sea salt and cracked black pepper
800g asparagus, trimmed⁺
400g feta, sliced

Place the oil, vinegar, dill, tarragon, chives, garlic, salt and
pepper in a small bowl and mix to combine.

Place the asparagus in a large saucepan of salted boiling
water and cook for 1 minute or until just tender. Drain and
refresh under cold running water. Arrange on a serving plate.
Top with the feta and drizzle with dressing to serve. SERVES 8
+ To trim asparagus, either remove the woody end by bending the
stalk at the base until it snaps, or shave off the tough outer skin
using a vegetable peeler. Cut with a knife to make a neat edge.

greens with sage butter

700g green beans, trimmed
4 x 175g bunches broccolini (tenderstem), trimmed
sage butter
150g unsalted butter, chopped
1 bunch sage (about 6 sprigs), leaves picked
sea salt and cracked black pepper

Place the beans and broccolini in a large saucepan of
salted boiling water and cook for 2 minutes or until tender.
Drain, refresh under cold running water and set aside.

To make the sage butter, melt the butter in a large
non-stick frying pan over medium heat. Add the sage and
cook for 3–4 minutes or until crispy.

Add the beans, broccolini, salt and pepper and toss until
warmed through.

Arrange the greens on a serving plate and spoon the
sage butter over to serve. SERVES 8

roast potatoes with green beans and speck

1.5kg kipfler (waxy) potatoes, halved lengthways
300g speck, chopped
2 tablespoons extra virgin olive oil
300g green beans, trimmed and blanched
mustard dressing
¼ cup (60ml) extra virgin olive oil
1 tablespoon white wine vinegar
1 tablespoon lemon juice
1 tablespoon Dijon mustard
sea salt and cracked black pepper

Preheat oven to 180°C (350°F).

Place the potato, speck and oil in a roasting pan, sprinkle
with salt and toss to coat. Roast, turning occasionally, for
40 minutes or until golden.

To make the mustard dressing, place the oil, vinegar,
lemon juice, mustard, salt and pepper in a bowl and whisk
to combine.

Add the beans to the potatoes. Top with the dressing and
toss to combine. Transfer to a serving platter to serve. SERVES 8

brussels sprout, broad bean and almond salad

2 tablespoons extra virgin olive oil
80g unsalted butter
2 cloves garlic, crushed
750g Brussels sprouts, sliced
1 cup (120g) frozen peas, thawed
1 cup (140g) broad (fava) beans, peeled and blanched
sea salt and cracked black pepper
⅓ cup (45g) slivered almonds
⅓ cup sage leaves
1 tablespoon finely grated lemon rind

Heat half the oil and the butter in a large non-stick frying pan over high heat. Add the garlic and Brussels sprout and cook, stirring occasionally, for 2–3 minutes or until golden. Add the peas and broad beans and cook for a further 1–2 minutes. Sprinkle with salt and pepper, transfer to a serving plate and keep warm.

Add the remaining oil, the almonds and sage to the pan and cook, stirring, for 1 minute or until golden. Add the lemon rind, toss to combine and spoon onto the greens to serve. SERVES 4–6

potato, apple and horseradish mash

1.5kg sebago (starchy) potatoes, peeled and roughly chopped
6 Granny Smith (green) apples, peeled, cored and chopped
40g unsalted butter
1½ tablespoons grated fresh horseradish
sea salt and cracked black pepper
⅓ cup (80g) crème fraîche

Place the potato in a large saucepan of cold, salted water. Bring to the boil and cook for 15 minutes. Add the apple and cook for a further 8 minutes or until the potato and apple are tender. Drain well, return to the pan and mash until smooth. Add the butter, horseradish and salt and mix to combine.

Place the mash in a serving bowl and top with the crème fraîche. Sprinkle with pepper to serve. SERVES 4–6

zucchini salad with honey lemon dressing

300g zucchini (courgette), thinly sliced using a mandoline
400g yellow squash, thinly sliced using a mandoline
2 cups mint leaves
½ cup (40g) shaved ricotta salata+ or parmesan
sea salt and cracked black pepper
honey lemon dressing
¼ cup (60ml) extra virgin olive oil
2 tablespoons lemon juice
2 teaspoons honey

To make the honey lemon dressing, place the oil, lemon
juice and honey in a small jug and whisk to combine.
   Place the zucchini, squash, mint and ricotta salata on a
serving plate. Drizzle with the honey lemon dressing and
sprinkle with salt and pepper to serve. **SERVES 4–6**
+ *Ricotta salata is a hard, salted ricotta that has been aged
and dried. Find it at delicatessens and Italian grocery stores.*
*Tip: If you don't have a mandoline, you can use a peeler to
thinly slice the vegetables.*

baked parsnip, sweet potato and gruyère mash

750g sweet potatoes (kumara), peeled and chopped
750g parsnips, peeled and chopped
30g unsalted butter
¼ cup (60g) sour cream
1 cup (125g) finely grated gruyère
sea salt and cracked black pepper
2 eggs
1½ cups (100g) fresh brioche or sourdough breadcrumbs
1 clove garlic, crushed
1 tablespoon extra virgin olive oil
2 tablespoons thyme or lemon thyme leaves

Preheat oven to 180°C (350°F).
   Place the potato and parsnip in a large saucepan of boiling
water and cook for 10–15 minutes or until tender. Drain and
return to the pan. Add the butter, sour cream, gruyère, salt
and pepper and mash until smooth. Add the eggs, 1 at a time,
and mix well. Spoon into a 1.5-litre-capacity baking dish.
Place the breadcrumbs, garlic and oil in a small bowl and mix
to combine. Sprinkle onto the mash and bake for 10 minutes
or until golden. Top with thyme to serve. **SERVES 4–6**

treats

Whimsical puffs of meringue, sugar-spun caramels, soft gingerbread and shimmering trifle – it must be Christmas! I do love the special kind of magic that comes with this time of year, and for me, nothing captures it quite like baking treats. Be they show-stopping desserts, charming gifts or edible decorations, I think festive sweets bring everyone joy, young and old. All my favourite recipes are here – I'll guide you through the classics, like brandy-soaked fruit cake and cloth-wrapped pudding, to more modern pavlova and trifle ideas, to cookies that are fit for a certain midnight visitor.

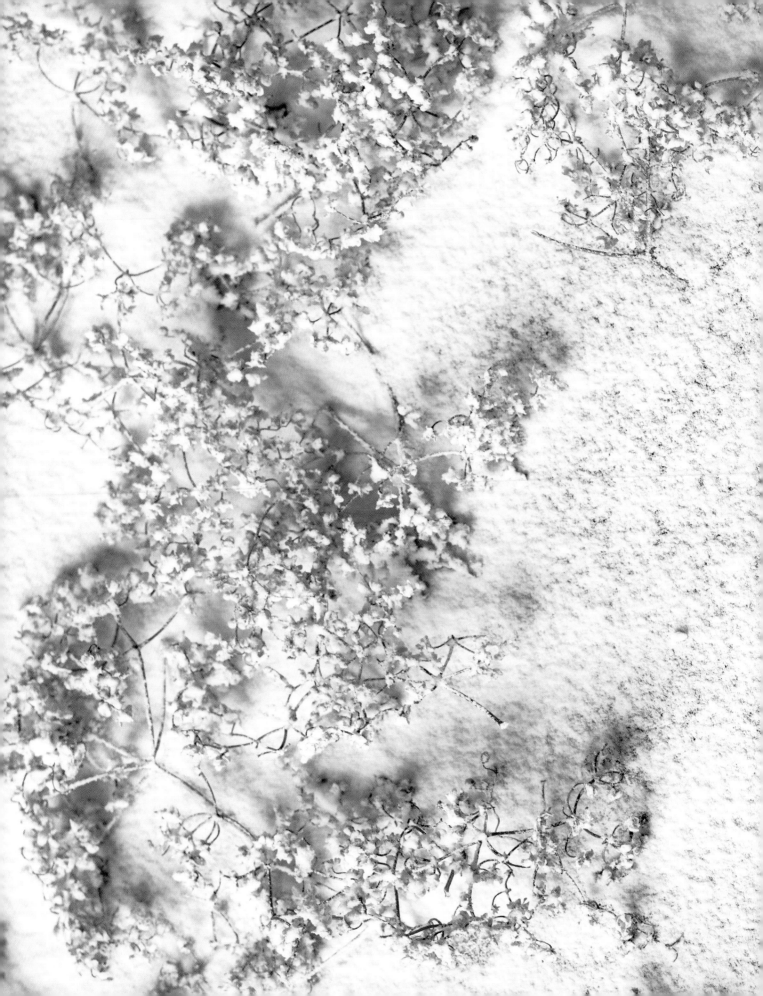

cakes and desserts

For some, it isn't Christmas without a fruit-laced cake.
From traditional treats to spiced up and reimagined versions
of loved classics, and festive sweets from around the world,
these dazzling desserts will make a grand finale.

pour in the brandy

add the dry ingredients

add the butter mixture

mix well to combine

spread evenly in the tin

christmas cake

3 cups (495g) raisins
1½ cups (240g) sultanas
1 cup (135g) dried currants
8 soft fresh dates (160g), pitted and chopped
1 cup (140g) slivered almonds
¾ cup (180ml) brandy[+]
250g unsalted butter, softened
1¼ cups (300g) firmly packed brown sugar
4 eggs
2¼ cups (335g) plain (all-purpose) flour, sifted
¼ teaspoon bicarbonate of (baking) soda
1½ teaspoons ground cinnamon
1 teaspoon ground allspice
2–3 tablespoons brandy[+], extra

Place the raisins, sultanas, currants, dates and almonds in a large bowl. Add the brandy, mix to combine and cover. Allow to soak in a cool dark place overnight, mixing occasionally.

Preheat oven to 140°C (275°F). Line a 20cm square cake tin with 2 layers of non-stick baking paper.

Place the butter and sugar in the bowl of an electric mixer and beat on medium speed for 8 minutes or until pale and creamy. Add the eggs, 1 at a time, beating well after each addition. Set aside.

Add the flour, bicarbonate of soda, cinnamon and allspice to the soaked fruit and mix well, ensuring the fruit is evenly coated with flour. Add the butter mixture and stir until well combined. Spoon into the tin and smooth the top. Bake for 2 hours or until cooked when tested with a skewer.

Spoon over the extra brandy while the cake is still warm. Allow to cool completely in the tin, before turning out onto a cake stand or plate to serve. SERVES 16–24
+ *While brandy is the traditional partner for fruit cake, you could also try using a dessert sherry such as Pedro Ximénez. It's an intensely sweet, dark sherry made from the Spanish grape variety of the same name. Perfect in festive cakes, puddings and custards, you can find it in liquor stores.*
Tip: Store this cake in an airtight container in a cool, dark place for up to 2 months.

christmas cake

cook's tips

○ The Christmas cake does benefit from long soaking of the fruit. You could macerate the fruit for 24 hours or even longer, if time permits, for a richer flavour.

○ You can use your favourite variety of brandy, sweet sherry or rum to soak the fruit and top the cake.

○ Double-lining the cake tin with non-stick baking paper ensures the cake doesn't become too dark during its long time in the oven.

○ The extra brandy should be spooned over the cake while it's still warm, as the cake will soak up more liquid as it cools.

○ You can make this cake up to 4 weeks in advance.

snowy christmas fruit cake

1 x quantity Christmas cake mixture (see *recipe*, page 124)
gingerbread snowmen (see *recipe*, page 236) and twigs,
    for decorating
icing (confectioner's) sugar, for dusting
icing
2 cups (320g) icing (confectioner's) sugar, sifted
1–1½ tablespoons boiling water

Preheat oven to 140°C (275°F). Line a 20cm round tin (10cm deep) with 2 layers of non-stick baking paper.
  Spoon the cake mixture into the tin. Bake for 2 hours or until cooked when tested with a skewer. Spoon over the extra brandy while the cake is still warm. Allow to cool completely in the tin.
  To make the icing, place the sugar and water in a medium bowl and mix to combine.
  Turn the cake out onto a cake stand or plate. Spoon on the icing and smooth with a palette knife. Dust the snowmen with sugar and place on the cake. Add the twigs to serve.
SERVES 16-24

cranberry and fig bundt cakes with gingerbread antlers

cranberry and fig bundt cakes with gingerbread antlers

¾ cup (100g) dried cranberries
¾ cup (110g) raisins
½ cup (80g) dried currants
¾ cup (150g) dried figs, chopped
½ cup (50g) flaked almonds
½ cup (125ml) brandy, plus 2 tablespoons extra
150g unsalted butter, softened
¾ cup (180g) firmly packed brown sugar
2 eggs
1¼ cups (185g) plain (all-purpose) flour, sifted
¼ teaspoon bicarbonate of (baking) soda, sifted
1 teaspoon mixed spice
¼ cup (60ml) milk
6 gingerbread antlers, for decorating (see *recipe*, page 236)
icing (confectioner's) sugar, for dusting
24 sprigs lemon thyme, for decorating

Place the cranberries, raisins, currants, figs, almonds and brandy in a medium saucepan over medium heat. Cook, stirring occasionally, for 8 minutes or until the fruit is plump and the brandy has been absorbed. Allow to cool completely.

Preheat oven to 140°C (275°F). Grease 6 x 1-cup-capacity (250ml) mini bundt tins.

Place the butter and sugar in the bowl of an electric mixer and beat for 6–8 minutes or until pale and creamy. Add the eggs, 1 at a time, beating well after each addition. Place the fruit mixture, flour, bicarbonate of soda and mixed spice in a large bowl and mix well to combine, coating the fruit in the flour. Add the butter mixture and the milk and mix to combine. Divide between the tins and place on a large baking tray. Bake for 30 minutes or until cooked when tested with a skewer. Allow to cool in the tins for 5 minutes before turning out onto a wire rack. Drizzle with the extra brandy and allow to cool completely.

Place onto cake stands or plates and top with the gingerbread antlers. Dust with icing sugar and decorate with lemon thyme to serve. MAKES 6

spiced sticky date, caramel and star-anise cakes

20 soft fresh dates (400g), pitted and chopped
1½ cups (375ml) boiling water
1½ teaspoons bicarbonate of (baking) soda
150g unsalted butter, chopped
1 cup (240g) firmly packed brown sugar
3 eggs
1½ cups (225g) self-raising (self-rising) flour
2 teaspoons ground cinnamon
2 teaspoons mixed spice
1⅓ cups (400g) store-bought good-quality dulce de leche[+]
star-anise, for decorating

Preheat oven to 160°C (325°F). Line 2 x 12cm round cake tins with non-stick baking paper, allowing 2cm of paper to extend above the edges.

Place the dates, water and bicarbonate of soda in a medium heatproof bowl and allow to soak for 10 minutes. Place the date mixture, butter and sugar in a food processor and process until well combined. Add the eggs, flour, cinnamon and mixed spice and process until just combined. Divide the mixture between the tins. Bake for 55 minutes–1 hour or until cooked when tested with a skewer. Allow to cool in the tins for 10 minutes before turning out onto a wire rack to cool completely.

Trim the tops from the cakes, using a large serrated knife. Place each cake onto a cake stand or plate. Using a small palette knife, spread the dulce de leche evenly over the top and sides of the cakes. Decorate with star-anise[++]. SERVES 6–8
+ Use a good-quality, thick dulce de leche, available in select supermarkets and grocers.
++ The star-anise in this recipe are simply for decoration – you can remove them from the cakes before eating.

spiced sticky date, caramel and star-anise cakes

rum and raisin brownie christmas trees

rum and raisin brownie christmas trees

1½ cups (245g) raisins
¾ cup (180ml) dark rum
200g dark (70% cocoa) chocolate, chopped
250g unsalted butter, chopped
1¾ cups (420g) firmly packed brown sugar
4 eggs
1⅓ cups (200g) plain (all-purpose) flour
¼ teaspoon baking powder
⅓ cup (35g) cocoa
cinnamon sticks and star-anise, for decorating
icing
1 cup (160g) icing (confectioner's) sugar, sifted
2–3 teaspoons boiling water

Preheat oven to 180°C (350°F). Line a 24cm x 34cm slice tin with non-stick baking paper.

Place the raisins and rum in a small saucepan over medium heat. Cook, stirring occasionally, for 8–10 minutes or until the liquid has been absorbed. Mash roughly with a fork and set aside.

Place the chocolate and butter in a medium saucepan over low heat and stir until melted and smooth. Remove from the heat and place in a large bowl. Add the sugar, eggs, flour, baking powder and cocoa and whisk well to combine. Add the raisin mixture and mix to combine. Pour into the tin and bake for 20–22 minutes or until cooked when tested with a skewer. Allow to cool completely in the tin. Turn out and, using a 9cm tree-shaped cutter, cut 10 trees from the brownie.

To make the icing, place the sugar and water in a small bowl and mix to combine.

Spoon the icing into a piping bag fitted with a small round nozzle and pipe the icing onto the trees. Decorate with the cinnamon and star-anise to serve[+]. **MAKES 10**
+ *Remove the cinnamon sticks and star-anise before eating.*

hazelnut forest cake with cream cheese icing

225g unsalted butter, chopped and softened
1½ cups (360g) firmly packed brown sugar
2 teaspoons vanilla extract
6 eggs
2¼ cups (335g) self-raising (self-rising) flour, sifted
2¼ cups (225g) hazelnut meal (ground hazelnuts)
1 teaspoon ground cinnamon
½ cup (125ml) milk
¼ cup (60ml) brandy or fresh orange juice, plus
    2 tablespoons extra for brushing
gingerbread reindeer, for decorating (see *recipe*, page 244)
1 cup (160g) icing (confectioner's) sugar, sifted, plus extra
2–2½ teaspoons boiling water
3 thick sprigs rosemary
cream cheese icing
500g cream cheese, chopped and softened
100g unsalted butter, chopped and softened
2 cups (320g) icing (confectioner's) sugar, sifted
2 teaspoons vanilla extract

Preheat oven to 160°C (325°F). Line 2 x 18cm round cake tins with non-stick baking paper.

Place the butter, brown sugar and vanilla in the bowl of an electric mixer and beat for 5–6 minutes or until pale and creamy. Add the eggs, 1 at a time, beating well after each addition. Add the flour, hazelnut meal, cinnamon, milk and brandy or orange juice and beat on low speed until just combined. Divide the mixture evenly between the tins. Bake for 55 minutes–1 hour or until cooked when tested with a skewer. Allow to cool in the tins for 10 minutes, before turning out onto a wire rack to cool completely.

To make the cream cheese icing, place the cream cheese, butter, sugar and vanilla in the clean bowl of an electric mixer. Beat for 8 minutes or until pale and fluffy[+].

To assemble, trim the tops and slice each cake in half horizontally, using a large serrated knife. Brush each layer with the extra brandy or orange juice. Place 1 of the cake bases on a cake stand or plate and spread with ⅔ cup (160ml) of the icing. Repeat the process, finishing with the remaining icing.

Combine the icing sugar and boiling water. Spoon into a piping bag fitted with a small round nozzle and pipe spots onto each reindeer. Top the cake with the rosemary and the reindeer and dust with the extra icing sugar. **SERVES 10–12**
+ *Place the cream cheese icing in the refrigerator for 15 minutes if it needs to firm up slightly.*

hazelnut forest cake
with cream cheese icing

cranberry and pistachio pannettone

cranberry and pistachio panettone

2½ teaspoons dry yeast
⅓ cup (80ml) lukewarm milk
½ cup (110g) raw caster (superfine) sugar
1 cup (140g) dried cranberries, chopped
1 cup (250ml) boiling water
4 eggs
1 tablespoon vanilla extract
3 cups (450g) plain (all-purpose) flour, plus extra for dusting
275g unsalted butter, chopped and softened slightly
⅔ cup (100g) unsalted shelled pistachios, roughly chopped
1½ tablespoons coarsely grated orange rind

Place the yeast, milk and 2 teaspoons of the sugar in a bowl and mix to combine. Allow to stand in a warm place for 10 minutes or until the surface is foamy.

Place the cranberries in a heatproof bowl. Cover with the boiling water and set aside to soak.

Place the eggs, vanilla, yeast mixture, flour and remaining sugar into the bowl of a stand mixer with the dough hook attached and mix to combine. Add the butter, a few cubes at a time, beating well after each addition.

Drain the cranberries and dry on absorbent kitchen paper. Add the cranberries, pistachio and orange rind to the dough mixture and beat for 1 minute or until well combined. Transfer to a lightly oiled bowl and allow to stand for 2 hours or until doubled in size.

Preheat oven to 220°C (425°F). Grease 6 x 1-cup-capacity (250ml) tins or dariole moulds. Line the bases and sides with non-stick baking paper, letting the paper extend 2cm above the rim of the tins.

Divide the dough into 6 pieces. Lightly dust the bench with flour and roll the dough pieces into balls. Press the balls into the tins and place on a large baking tray. Cover with a damp tea towel and allow to stand for 30–40 minutes or until risen. Remove the tea towel and reduce the oven temperature to 180°C (350°F). Bake for 25 minutes or until golden and cooked through. Allow to cool for 5 minutes, before removing from the tins. Serve immediately or place on a wire rack to cool completely. MAKES 6

Tip: We've baked these panettone in clean BPA-free tin cans. We used small food cans with straight sides so you could easily give the panettone in its tin can as a gift. For a pretty finishing touch, wrap the tin cans with a piece of hessian or ribbon and secure with a wooden peg.

Let the caramelised flavours and *incredible creaminess* of this 'burnt' cheesecake tempt you to break with dessert traditions this Christmas. *You'll never look at cheesecake* the same way again!

Basque burnt cheesecake

starry apple and cranberry pie

1 tablespoon caster (superfine) sugar
sweet shortcrust pastry
4 cups (600g) plain (all-purpose) flour
350g cold unsalted butter, chopped
½ cup (80g) icing (confectioner's) sugar, sifted
2 egg yolks
⅓ cup (80ml) iced water
apple and cranberry filling
3 pink lady (red) apples, peeled and chopped
2 cups (220g) frozen cranberries
3 cups (375g) frozen raspberries
½ cup (120g) firmly packed brown sugar
20g unsalted butter
½ teaspoon ground cinnamon
1 teaspoon finely grated orange rind
1 tablespoon brandy
1 tablespoon cornflour (cornstarch)

To make the sweet shortcrust pastry, place the flour, cold butter and icing sugar in a food processor and pulse until the mixture resembles fine breadcrumbs. With the motor running, add the egg yolks and water and process until the dough just comes together. Turn out onto a lightly floured surface and gently bring together to form a ball. Divide in half and flatten each portion to create 2 discs. Roll each disc out between 2 sheets of non-stick baking paper to 4mm thick and refrigerate for 1 hour.

Meanwhile, to make the apple and cranberry filling, place the apple, cranberries, raspberries, brown sugar, butter, cinnamon and orange rind in a large saucepan over medium heat. Combine the brandy and cornflour in a small bowl and stir into the apple mixture. Cook, stirring, for 5–7 minutes or until the mixture is slightly thickened. Set aside to cool slightly, then refrigerate for 1 hour or until chilled.

Preheat oven to 180°C (350°F).

Remove the paper from 1 sheet of pastry and place the pastry into an 18cm metal pie dish. Remove the top layer of paper from the second sheet of pastry (it should still have a sheet of paper underneath it). Use a 3cm star pastry cutter to cut out 10 stars from the centre of the pastry[+]. Reserve the stars.

Spoon the chilled cranberry filling into the pie case. Place the second pastry sheet over the top, positioning the star cut-outs to fit within the dish. Trim the excess pastry and reserve. Press the pastry edges together to seal them.

Bring all the excess pastry together into a flattened disc. Roll out between 2 sheets of non-stick baking paper to 4mm thick. Use the 3cm star pastry cutter to cut out about 28 stars. Arrange the stars, including the reserved stars, along the edge of the pie, overlapping them slightly. Sprinkle with the caster sugar and bake for 45–50 minutes or until golden brown. Allow to cool slightly and serve.

SERVES 8

+ *Allow a border of 5cm on the pie top before cutting out the stars.*

basque burnt cheesecake

750g cream cheese, chopped and softened
1 cup (220g) caster (superfine) sugar
4 large eggs
1½ cups (375ml) double (thick) cream
1 teaspoon vanilla bean paste
1½ tablespoons plain (all-purpose) flour or rice flour

Preheat oven to 220°C (425°F). Line a 22cm springform tin with an inverted base, or a 22cm skillet, with 3 large sheets of overlapping non-stick baking paper, ensuring the paper extends high above the rim[+].

Place the cream cheese and sugar in the bowl of an electric mixer. Using the whisk attachment, beat until smooth and soft peaks form. Add the eggs, one at a time, beating after each addition, until combined.

Add the cream and vanilla and beat until just combined. Sift in the flour and beat on low speed, until thickened. Pour into the tin and bake for 15 minutes, then rotate and bake for a further 10–15 minutes[++]. The cheesecake should rise up like a soufflé and caramelise, almost burning on the top, but still have an extreme wiggle in the middle.

Once out of the oven, allow to cool for 1 hour (the cheesecake will sink a bit), then refrigerate until chilled.

SERVES 10

+ *The triple layer of baking paper that extends high above the tin protects the sides from burning.*
++ *We used one quantity of the cheesecake mixture to make 2 smaller cheesecakes. These were made in 2 x 16cm skillets. Bake for 8 minutes, rotate, then cook for a further 10 minutes.*

starry apple and cranberry pie

Fluffy clouds of meringue conceal the *prettiest angel cake* that's layered with *fresh raspberry-rippled* meringue.

cloud cake

450ml eggwhite (about 12 eggs), at room temperature
  (see *cook's tips*, page 151)
1 teaspoon cream of tartar
1¼ cups (275g) caster (superfine) sugar
2 teaspoons vanilla extract
1 cup (150g) plain (all-purpose) flour
250g raspberries, torn
Italian meringue
⅓ cup (80ml) water
½ teaspoon cream of tartar
2 cups (440g) caster (superfine) sugar
150ml eggwhite (about 4 eggs), at room temperature

Preheat oven to 180°C (350°F).

Place the eggwhite and cream of tartar in the bowl of an electric mixer and whisk on high speed until soft peaks form. Gradually add ¾ cup (165g) of the sugar and the vanilla, whisking until thick and glossy.

Sift the flour and the remaining ½ cup (110g) of sugar into a bowl. Sift a second time, then sift a third time over the eggwhite mixture. Using a metal spoon, gently fold to combine. Spoon into an ungreased 21cm round angel food cake tin and smooth the top. Bake for 30 minutes or until the cake comes away from the sides of the tin. Invert the tin onto its feet and allow to cool for 1 hour.

Using a palette knife, gently loosen the sides of the cake and twist the middle funnel to lift it from the tin. Using a large serrated knife, slice the cake horizontally into 3 even layers.

To make the Italian meringue, place the water, cream of tartar and 1 cup (220g) of the sugar in a small saucepan over high heat. Cook, stirring, until the sugar is dissolved. Bring to the boil, reduce the heat to medium and cook for 4 minutes. Place the eggwhite in the clean bowl of an electric mixer and whisk on high speed until stiff peaks form. With the motor running, gradually add the remaining 1 cup (220g) of sugar, 1 tablespoon at a time, whisking for 30 seconds before adding more. Gradually add the hot sugar syrup in a thin steady stream and whisk for a further 4 minutes or until thick, glossy and cooled. Place one-third of the Italian meringue into a separate bowl and stir through the raspberries.

To assemble, place 1 layer of cake on a cake stand or plate and top with half the raspberry Italian meringue. Repeat with the remaining cake and raspberry Italian meringue, finishing with a cake layer. Using a palette knife, spread the remaining Italian meringue over the cake. **SERVES 10–12**

+ *Store the cake in an airtight container for up to 24 hours.*

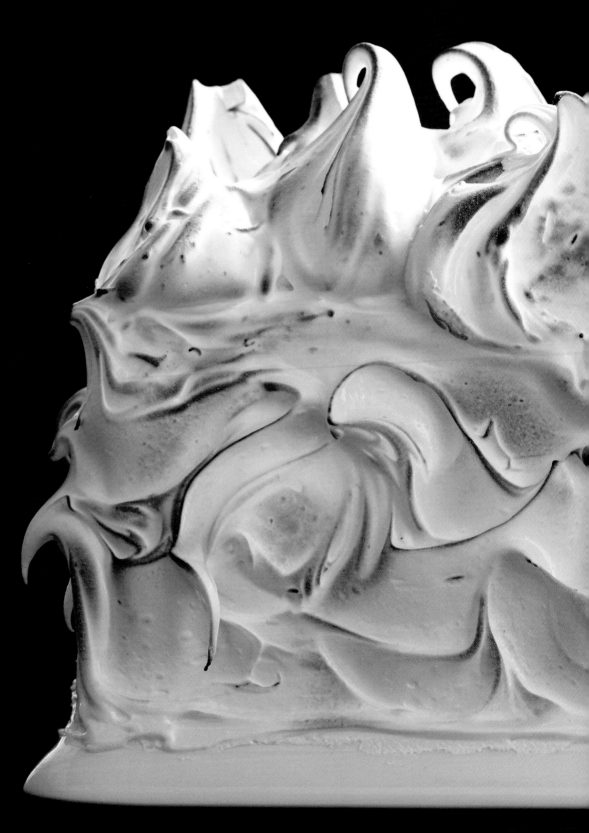

Beneath its *glossy Italian meringue* exterior lies a light gin spritz sponge cake with a *lemony ice-cream core.* Once bronzed, the soft meringue takes on a *crisp caramel flavour.*

gin spritz baked alaska

gin spritz baked alaska

2 x 450g store-bought rectangular plain vanilla
   sponge cakes, trimmed
1.5 litres store-bought vanilla bean ice-cream
1 cup (350g) store-bought lemon curd
gin spritz syrup
½ cup (110g) caster (superfine) sugar
¼ cup (60ml) lemon juice (about 2 lemons)
rind from 2 lemons, finely grated
¼ cup (60ml) gin
Italian meringue
⅓ cup (80ml) water
½ teaspoon cream of tartar
2 cups (440g) caster (superfine) sugar
150ml eggwhite (about 4 eggs), at room temperature
   (see *cook's tips*, page 151)

To make the gin spritz syrup, place the sugar, lemon juice
and rind in a small saucepan over medium heat, stirring, until
the sugar is dissolved. Cook for 2 minutes or until thickened
slightly. Stir in the gin and set aside to cool.

Line a 12-cup-capacity (11cm x 26cm) loaf tin with 2 layers
of plastic wrap. Cut the sponge cake into 2cm-thick slices
and use to line the base and sides of the tin, trimming the
sponge to fit snugly into the tin and reserving enough to
enclose. Drizzle with the gin spritz syrup and set aside.

Place the ice-cream in the bowl of an electric mixer and
beat until soft. Fold through the lemon curd. Working
quickly, spoon the ice-cream mixture into the sponge-lined
tin. Top with the reserved sponge cake and press to enclose.
Cover with plastic wrap and freeze for 6 hours or overnight.

To make the Italian meringue, place the water, cream of
tartar and 1 cup (220g) of the sugar in a small saucepan over
high heat. Cook, stirring, until the sugar is dissolved. Bring to
the boil, reduce the heat to medium and cook for 4 minutes.

Place the eggwhite in the clean bowl of an electric mixer
and whisk on high speed until stiff peaks form. With the
motor running, gradually add the remaining sugar,
1 tablespoon at a time, whisking for 30 seconds before
adding more. Gradually add the hot sugar syrup in a thin
steady stream and whisk for a further 4 minutes or until
the meringue is thick, glossy and cooled.

To serve, invert onto a serving platter and discard the
plastic wrap. Using a palette knife, spread the meringue over
the sponge. Use a small kitchen blowtorch to lightly toast the
meringue until golden brown. Serve immediately. **SERVES 12–14**

gingerbread and peanut caramel squares

175g unsalted butter, softened
1¼ cups (300g) firmly packed brown sugar
½ cup (175g) golden syrup
1 cup (250ml) pure cream
1½ cups (210g) unsalted peanuts
gingerbread
125g unsalted butter, softened
½ cup (120g) firmly packed brown sugar
⅔ cup (230g) golden syrup
2½ cups (375g) plain (all-purpose) flour, sifted
1 teaspoon bicarbonate of (baking) soda, sifted
2 teaspoons ground ginger
2 teaspoons mixed spice

To make the gingerbread, line a 20cm x 30cm slice tin
with non-stick baking paper, allowing 3cm of paper to
extend above the edges.

Place the butter and sugar in the bowl of an electric
mixer and beat for 5–6 minutes, scraping down the sides
of the bowl, until pale and creamy. Add the golden syrup,
flour, bicarbonate of soda, ginger and mixed spice and
beat until the mixture just comes together to form a dough.
Press the dough into the tin and refrigerate for 30 minutes
or until firm.

Preheat oven to 180°C (350°F).

Bake the gingerbread for 12–15 minutes or until golden.
Set aside to cool in the tin.

Place the butter, sugar and golden syrup in a medium
saucepan over medium heat and stir until melted and smooth.
Bring to the boil and cook for 8–10 minutes or until the
temperature reaches 140°C (284°F) on a sugar (candy)
thermometer. Gradually add the cream, stir to combine and
cook for 2 minutes. Add the peanuts and stir to combine.
Carefully pour the caramel onto the gingerbread base. Place
the tin on a large baking tray+ and bake for 15–18 minutes
or until dark golden and slightly set around the edges.
Allow to cool in the tin at room temperature for 10 minutes
before refrigerating until set.

Use the paper to help you lift the slice from the tin.
Using a sharp knife, trim the edges and cut the slice into
squares. Keep refrigerated until ready to serve. **MAKES 15**
+ *It's a good idea to place the tin on a large baking tray in case
the caramel bubbles over while cooking.*
*Tip: This slice will keep in the refrigerator for up to 2–3 days.
Bring it to room temperature to serve.*

gingerbread and peanut caramel squares

soak the fruit

add the butter mixture

flour the cloth

shape the mixture

tie with kitchen string

lower into the water

christmas pudding

¼ cup (40g) sultanas
½ cup (80g) dried currants
¾ cup (120g) raisins
8 soft fresh dates (160g), pitted and chopped
½ cup (70g) slivered almonds
½ teaspoon mixed spice
⅓ cup (80ml) sweet sherry
⅔ cup (160ml) brandy
125g unsalted butter, softened
¼ cup (60g) firmly packed brown sugar
¼ cup (55g) caster (superfine) sugar
2 eggs
⅔ cup (100g) plain (all-purpose) flour, sifted
1½ cups (100g) fresh white breadcrumbs
brandy custard (see *recipe*, page 149), to serve

Place the sultanas, currants, raisins, dates, almonds, mixed spice, sherry and half the brandy in a large bowl and mix to combine. Cover and allow to soak in a cool, dark place for 24 hours, mixing occasionally.

Place the butter and both the sugars in the bowl of an electric mixer and beat for 8–10 minutes or until pale and creamy. Add the eggs, 1 at a time, beating well after each addition. Add the butter mixture, half the flour and the breadcrumbs to the soaked fruit and mix to combine.

Place a large saucepan of water over high heat and bring to the boil. Add a 60cm-square piece of calico cloth and boil for 5 minutes. Using tongs, remove the calico and allow to cool. Squeeze to remove any excess water. Drain, refill the pan with water and bring to the boil. Open the calico out and top with the remaining ⅓ cup (50g) of flour. Rub the flour over the calico to form a large circle. Spoon the pudding mixture into the centre of the calico to form a mound and gather the ends together firmly. Tie the calico as close to the mixture as possible with kitchen string, leaving at least a 15cm length of string at both ends (see *cook's tips*, page 149). Place the pudding in the water, reduce the heat to medium and cover with a tight-fitting lid. Simmer for 4 hours, adding more water if necessary.

Drain and hang the pudding over a bowl for 24–48 hours or until dry. Cut the string and invert the pudding onto a serving plate. Gently remove the cloth, top with the remaining ⅓ cup (80ml) of brandy and serve with brandy custard. SERVES 6–8

christmas pudding

brandy custard

brandy custard

1½ cups (375ml) milk
1 vanilla bean, halved and seeds scraped
10 egg yolks
⅓ cup (50g) plain (all-purpose) flour
1 cup (160g) icing (confectioner's) sugar, sifted
⅔ cup (160ml) pure cream, whipped
¼ cup (60ml) brandy

Place the milk and vanilla bean and seeds in a medium saucepan over medium heat and bring just to the boil. Place the egg yolks, flour and sugar in the bowl of an electric mixer and whisk on medium speed until combined. With the motor running, gradually add the milk mixture, whisking until smooth.

Return the mixture to the saucepan over low heat and cook, whisking, for 12–15 minutes or until thickened. Strain into a heatproof bowl, cover the surface with plastic wrap (see *cook's tips*, right) and refrigerate until cold.

When ready to serve the custard, add the whipped cream and gently fold to combine. Add the brandy and stir to combine. Pour into a serving jug to serve. MAKES 3½ CUPS

cook's tips

∘ While English tradition would see families make their puddings on the last Sunday of November and hang them in a cool place until Christmas, warm Australian summers say otherwise! If the weather's warm, it's best to make this pudding up to 2 weeks in advance and store it in the refrigerator. You can reheat the pudding by boiling it for 1 hour or simply removing it from the cloth and microwaving it in single serves.

∘ The extra lengths of string tied to the pudding make lowering and lifting it a little easier. If your saucepan has two handles you could secure the ends of the string to them to stop the pudding from moving around and catching on the pan. Use the string to hang the pudding to dry, too.

∘ You can make the custard up to 3 days in advance, however add the whipped cream and brandy just before serving. By placing some plastic wrap over the custard while chilling, you'll prevent a 'skin' from forming on the surface.

classic pavlova

classic pavlova

225ml eggwhites (approximately 6 eggs), at room
    temperature (see *cook's tips*, right)
1½ cups (330g) caster (superfine) sugar
1½ teaspoons white vinegar
1½ cups (375ml) pure cream
125g raspberries
1⅔ cups (250g) white cherries[+], stems intact
icing (confectioner's) sugar, for dusting

Preheat oven to 150°C (300°F).

Place the eggwhite in the bowl of an electric mixer and whisk on high speed until stiff peaks form.

Gradually add the sugar, 1 tablespoon at a time, waiting 30 seconds between each addition. Once all the sugar has been added, scrape down the sides of the bowl with a spatula and whisk for a further 6 minutes or until the mixture is stiff and glossy.

Add the vinegar and whisk for 4 minutes or until glossy and combined.

Pile spoonfuls of the meringue onto a baking tray lined with non-stick baking paper and, using a spatula, shape to form a 20cm mound. Reduce the oven temperature to 120°C (250°F) and bake for 1 hour 30 minutes or until dry and crisp to the touch.

Turn the oven off and allow the pavlova to cool completely in the oven with the door closed. Place the cream in a bowl and whisk until soft peaks form.

Place the pavlova on a cake stand or plate and top with the cream, raspberries and cherries. Dust with icing sugar to serve. **SERVES 10**

+ *White cherries are available at some farmers' markets and greengrocers. If you can't find them, use regular cherries.*

cook's tips

○ Making meringue is a science – for success, be sure to measure the eggwhites carefully (as instructed in the recipe), remembering that egg sizes do vary.

○ When separating the eggs, take care to ensure no yolk escapes into the whites. Egg yolks contain fat, which can prevent the whites from whipping well. For this reason, it's also important to use very clean equipment to beat the eggwhites.

○ Be sure to use fresh, room-temperature eggs – this will help the eggwhites to become more voluminous when beaten.

○ When the mixture is 'stiff and glossy', the sugar should be completely dissolved. To test this, simply rub a little of the mixture between your fingertips. If it feels gritty, continue to whisk.

○ To shape meringue into measured rounds for desserts like pavlova and baked Alaska, draw circles on the non-stick baking paper to guide you. Use a pencil, then place the paper pencil-side down on the tray to ensure no marks transfer to the meringue.

○ To avoid cracking larger meringues and pavlovas as you move them onto cake stands or plates, use the baking paper below to help you and simply trim any visible paper before serving. You could also try baking meringue on an ovenproof serving plate.

raspberry and eggnog baked alaska

150ml eggwhite (about 4 eggs), at room temperature
  (see *cook's tips*, page 151)
1½ cups (240g) icing (confectioner's) sugar, sifted
500ml store-bought raspberry sorbet, softened
1 litre store-bought vanilla bean ice-cream
½ cup (140g) store-bought thick vanilla bean custard
¼ teaspoon grated nutmeg
¼ teaspoon ground cinnamon
meringue icing
1½ cups (330g) caster (superfine) sugar
¼ teaspoon cream of tartar
½ cup (125ml) water
150ml eggwhite (about 4 eggs), at room temperature

Preheat oven to 120°C (250°F). Draw an 18cm circle on
2 sheets of non-stick baking paper (see *cook's tips*, page 151)
and place each on a separate baking tray.

Place the eggwhite in the bowl of an electric mixer and
whisk on high speed until stiff peaks form. Add the icing
sugar, 1 tablespoon at a time, whisking for 30 seconds
before adding more. Scrape down the sides of the bowl
and beat for a further 6 minutes or until stiff and glossy.
Spoon into a piping bag fitted with a 2cm round nozzle.
Pipe the meringue onto the trays in a spiral to fill in the
circles, leaving 5mm of room to spread. Bake for 1 hour or
until just crisp. Turn the oven off and allow the meringues
to cool in the oven with the door closed for 30 minutes.

Line a deep-sided loose-based 20cm round tin with
non-stick baking paper. Place 1 meringue round in the
base of the tin[+]. Spoon in the sorbet and spread evenly.
Freeze for 30 minutes or until just set.

Scoop the ice-cream into the clean bowl of an electric
mixer and beat on low speed for 1 minute or until softened.
Add the custard, nutmeg and cinnamon and beat to
combine. Spoon into the tin, reserving 1 cup (250ml), and
spread evenly. Top with the remaining meringue round
and spread with the reserved ice-cream mixture. Freeze for
6 hours or overnight, until frozen.

To make the meringue icing, place 1¼ cups (275g) of
the caster sugar, the cream of tartar and water in a small
saucepan over high heat and stir with a metal spoon until
just combined. Bring to the boil, reduce the heat to
medium and cook for 4 minutes. Place the eggwhite in
the clean bowl of an electric mixer and whisk on high speed
until soft peaks form. Add the remaining ¼ cup (55g) sugar
in 2 batches and whisk until stiff peaks form. With the
motor running, add the sugar syrup in a thin, steady stream
and whisk for 2–3 minutes or until thick and glossy.

Remove the cake from the tin and place on a cake stand
or plate. Spread the icing over the top and sides, using a
palette knife to create swirls and peaks. Use a small kitchen
blowtorch to brown the icing to serve[++]. **SERVES 8–10**
+ *If the meringue rounds for the baked Alaska are too large,
trim them with a small sharp knife to fit the tin.*
++ *You can serve the baked Alaska immediately, or keep it,
un-iced, in the freezer for up to 3 days. Make the meringue
icing before serving, remove the cake from the tin, then ice
and brown the meringue as instructed.*

raspberry and eggnog baked alaska

centrepiece pavlova

280ml eggwhite (about 8 eggs), at room temperature
   (see *cook's tips*, page 151)
2¼ cups (500g) caster (superfine) sugar
¼ teaspoon cream of tartar
125g blackberries or blueberries
125g cherries, pitted and halved
chocolate swirl cream
50g dark (70% cocoa) chocolate, chopped
¼ cup (60ml) pure cream
300ml double (thick) cream

Preheat oven to 150°C (300°F). Line a large flat baking
tray with non-stick baking paper.

Place the eggwhite, sugar and cream of tartar in a
heatproof glass bowl over a saucepan of simmering water
(the bowl shouldn't touch the water). Stir gently with a
spatula for 5 minutes, scraping down the sides of the bowl
to ensure all the sugar is dissolved+. Remove from the heat.

Transfer the mixture to the bowl of an electric mixer.
Beat for 8–10 minutes or until thick, glossy and cooled.

Spoon the meringue mixture onto the prepared tray to
make a 12cm x 30cm rectangle shape.

Reduce the oven temperature to 120°C (250°F) and
bake for 1 hour–1 hour 15 minutes or until dry and crisp
to the touch. Turn the oven off and allow the meringue to
cool completely in the oven with the door closed.

To make the chocolate swirl cream, place the chocolate
and pure cream in a small saucepan over low heat and stir
until melted and combined. Set aside to cool.

Place the double cream in a large bowl and whisk until
soft peaks form. Add the chocolate mixture and swirl
through with a metal spoon.

To serve, place the pavlova on a serving platter and top
with the chocolate swirl cream, the berries and cherries++.
SERVES 8–10
+ *Rub some of the eggwhite mixture between your fingertips
to ensure all the sugar is dissolved.*
++ *If you want to make multiple pavlovas, like we have done,
make 1 pavlova at a time and store them in an airtight
container in a cool, dry place (not the refrigerator).*

peach and raspberry meringue tart

2 sheets store-bought fresh or thawed frozen
    filo (phyllo) pastry
100g unsalted butter, melted
½ cup (110g) caster (superfine) sugar, plus 2 tablespoons extra
¼ cup (90g) honey
1 vanilla bean, split and seeds scraped
300g peaches, halved and cut into 1cm-thick slices
250g raspberries
meringue topping
225ml eggwhite (about 6 eggs), at room temperature
    (see *cook's tips*, page 151)
1½ cups (330g) caster (superfine) sugar
1½ teaspoons white vinegar

Preheat oven to 140°C (275°F). Line a 24cm x 36cm Swiss roll tin with non-stick baking paper.

Brush 1 sheet of pastry with butter, sprinkle with 2 teaspoons of the sugar and top with another sheet of pastry. Repeat with the remaining butter, sugar and pastry, finishing with a layer of sugar.

Place the pastry stack in the tin. Bake for 20–25 minutes or until golden[+]. Set aside.

Place a large non-stick frying pan over high heat. Add the extra sugar, the honey, vanilla seeds and peaches. Cook, stirring frequently, for 1–2 minutes or until the peaches are just soft. Add the raspberries and toss to combine. Set aside.

To make the meringue topping, place the eggwhite in the bowl of an electric mixer and whisk on high speed until stiff peaks form. Add the sugar, 1 tablespoon at a time, whisking for 30 seconds before adding more. Whisk for a further 6 minutes or until stiff and glossy. Scrape down the sides of the bowl, add the vinegar and whisk for 2 minutes or until glossy.

Preheat oven grill (broiler) to high heat. Spoon the meringue into a piping bag fitted with a 2cm round nozzle. Spoon the fruit onto the pastry, reserving the juices. Pipe the meringue onto the fruit and place the tart under the grill for 2–3 minutes or until just golden. Carefully remove the tart from the tin. Drizzle with the reserved juices and slice to serve. **SERVES 8–10**

[+] *The pastry will puff up in the oven, then deflate once it begins to cool.*

peach and raspberry meringue tart

cinnamon and candied pecan pavlova

cinnamon and candied pecan pavlova

150ml eggwhite (about 4 eggs), at room temperature
(see *cook's tips*, page 151)
1 cup (220g) caster (superfine) sugar
1 teaspoon white vinegar
1 cup (250ml) pure cream
1½ cups (375g) crème fraîche
¼ cup (40g) icing (confectioner's) sugar, plus extra for dusting
1 teaspoon ground cinnamon, plus extra for dusting
candied pecans
1 cup (120g) pecans, toasted
2 tablespoons caster (superfine) sugar
2 tablespoons brown sugar
2 teaspoons vanilla extract
¼ cup (60ml) whisky

Preheat oven to 150°C (300°F).

Place the eggwhite in the bowl of an electric mixer and whisk on high speed until stiff peaks form. Add the caster sugar, 1 tablespoon at a time, whisking for 30 seconds before adding more. Whisk for a further 6 minutes or until stiff and glossy. Scrape down the sides of the bowl, add the vinegar and whisk for 2 minutes or until glossy and combined. Draw a 26cm circle on a sheet of non-stick baking paper (see *cook's tips*, page 151) and place on a large baking tray. Spoon 1 cup (250ml) of the meringue into the centre of the circle, leaving a 5cm border. Arrange heaped spoonfuls of the remaining meringue in the border to create a ring. Reduce the oven temperature to 120°C (250°F) and bake for 1 hour 30 minutes or until crisp. Turn the oven off and allow the meringue to cool in the oven with the door closed for 1 hour 30 minutes.

To make the candied pecans, line a baking tray with non-stick baking paper. Place a small saucepan over medium heat. Add the pecans, both the sugars, the vanilla and whisky and cook, stirring occasionally in the last 1 minute, for 6–7 minutes or until golden and caramelised. Working quickly, carefully pour the mixture onto the tray. Spread and allow to cool completely. Roughly chop and set aside.

Place the cream, crème fraîche and the icing sugar in the clean bowl of an electric mixer and whisk until stiff peaks form. Add the cinnamon and fold to combine. Place the pavlova on a cake stand or plate, top the centre with the cream and sprinkle with the candied pecans. Dust with extra icing sugar and cinnamon to serve. **SERVES 8–10**

pandoro and vanilla baked alaska

1 x 1kg store-bought pandoro[+]
¼ cup (60ml) sloe gin[++]
3 litres store-bought vanilla bean ice-cream, softened
2 cups (250g) frozen raspberries
Italian meringue
⅓ cup (80ml) water
½ teaspoon cream of tartar
2 cups (440g) caster (superfine) sugar
150ml eggwhite (about 4 eggs), at room temperature
(see *cook's tips*, page 151)

Using a large serrated knife, slice about 2cm from the base of the pandoro. Using a 13cm round plate as a guide, trim and reserve the base. Using the same plate as a guide and leaving a 2cm-thick edge, cut into the underside of the cake and remove the centre to make a hollow. Brush the inside of the pandoro with the gin.

Line a baking tray with non-stick baking paper. Place the ice-cream and raspberries in a large bowl and mix to combine. Working quickly, spoon the ice-cream mixture into the hollow, top with the reserved base and press to secure. Place the pandoro, base-down, on the tray and freeze for 3–4 hours or until solid.

To make the Italian meringue, place the water, cream of tartar and 1 cup (220g) of the sugar in a small saucepan over high heat. Cook, stirring, until the sugar is dissolved. Bring to the boil, reduce the heat to medium and cook for 4 minutes. Place the eggwhite in the bowl of an electric mixer and whisk on high speed until stiff peaks form. With the motor running, add the remaining 1 cup (220g) of sugar, 1 tablespoon at a time, whisking for 30 seconds before adding more. Gradually add the hot sugar syrup in a thin steady stream and whisk for a further 4 minutes or until thick, glossy and cooled.

Place the pandoro on a cake stand or plate. Using a palette knife, spread the meringue over the pandoro. Using a small kitchen blowtorch, toast the meringue until golden brown. Serve immediately. **SERVES 8**

+ *Pandoro, meaning 'golden bread', is an Italian star-shaped sweet bread, available from delicatessens and Italian grocers. If you can't find pandoro, you can use plain or fruit panettone.*
++ *Sloe gin has a fruity flavour which complements this dessert well. If unavailable, simply omit it from the recipe.*

pandoro and vanilla baked alaska

raspberry swirl pavlova wreath

raspberry swirl pavlova wreath

225ml eggwhite (about 6 eggs), at room temperature
    (see *cook's tips*, page 151)
1½ cups (330g) caster (superfine) sugar
1½ teaspoons white vinegar
2 teaspoons cornflour (cornstarch)
1½ cups (375ml) pure cream
250g fresh raspberries
2 tablespoons shelled pistachios, finely chopped
1 tablespoon freeze-dried raspberries (optional),
    finely crushed+
raspberry swirl
½ cup (60g) frozen raspberries
2 tablespoons caster (superfine) sugar
1 teaspoon vanilla extract

To make the raspberry swirl, place the raspberries, sugar
and vanilla in a small saucepan over medium heat and cook,
stirring occasionally, for 3–4 minutes or until slightly reduced.
Strain into a heatproof bowl, discarding the seeds, and
refrigerate until cool.

Preheat oven to 150°C (300°F). Draw a 22cm circle on
a sheet of non-stick baking paper (see *cook's tips*, page 151)
and place it on a baking tray.

Place the eggwhite in the bowl of an electric mixer and
whisk on high speed until stiff peaks form. Gradually add
the sugar, 1 tablespoon at a time, whisking for 30 seconds
before adding more. Scrape down the sides of the bowl
and whisk for a further 6 minutes or until stiff and glossy.
Place the vinegar and cornflour in a small bowl and mix to
combine. Add to the meringue and whisk for 2 minutes or
until glossy and combined.

Place 12 heaped spoonfuls of the meringue mixture on
the tray around the inside of the circle to create a ring.
Drizzle the raspberry mixture over the meringue and use
a teaspoon to create a swirled effect. Reduce the oven
temperature to 120°C (250°F) and bake for 1 hour or until
crisp to the touch. Turn the oven off and allow the pavlova
to cool completely in the oven with the door closed.

Place the cream in the clean bowl of an electric mixer
and whisk until soft peaks form.

Place the pavlova wreath on a cake stand or plate. Top
with the cream and sprinkle with the raspberries, chopped
pistachios and freeze-dried raspberries to serve. SERVES 6–8
+ *Freeze-dried raspberries are available from select
delicatessens and specialty grocers.*

raspberry sweet bread wreath

1 teaspoon dry yeast
2 tablespoons caster (superfine) sugar
½ cup (125ml) lukewarm water
1½ tablespoons warm milk
1½ cups 00 (superfine) flour, plus extra for dusting
1½ tablespoons vegetable oil
¼ cup (40g) dried currants
1 tablespoon finely grated orange rind
1 teaspoon ground cinnamon
milk, for brushing
raw or Demerara sugar, for sprinkling
quick raspberry jam
1½ cups (185g) frozen raspberries
⅔ cup (150) caster (superfine) sugar

Place the yeast, caster sugar, water and milk in a medium
bowl and stir to combine. Set aside in a warm place for
5 minutes or until bubbles appear on the surface.

Place the flour, oil, currants, orange rind and cinnamon
in a large bowl and make a well in the centre. Add the yeast
mixture and mix to form a dough. Turn the dough out onto
a lightly floured surface and knead for 5–6 minutes or until
smooth and elastic. Place in a lightly oiled bowl, cover with
a clean, damp tea towel and allow to stand in a warm place
for 1 hour or until doubled in size.

While the dough is proving, make the quick raspberry
jam+. Place the raspberries and sugar in a medium non-stick
frying pan over high heat and stir until the sugar is dissolved.
Bring to the boil and cook, stirring, for 5–6 minutes or until
reduced and thickened slightly. Set aside to cool completely.

Preheat oven to 200°C (400°F).

Roll the dough out on a lightly floured surface to make a
rough 25cm x 55cm rectangle. Spread the dough with the
jam and roll up, starting from the long edge, to enclose.
Using a sharp knife, cut the rolled dough in half lengthways.
Join the top of the 2 pieces together and carefully slide onto
a sheet of non-stick baking paper. Twist the 2 lengths
together, form a wreath shape and join the ends. Gently
transfer the paper to a baking tray. Brush the wreath with
milk, sprinkle with raw sugar and bake for 15–20 minutes
or until golden and cooked through. Tie with a ribbon and
place in the centre of the table to serve. SERVES 10–12
+ *You could also use ½ cup (160g) store-bought raspberry jam.*

raspberry sweet bread wreath

smoked almond and cherry panforte

smoked almond and cherry panforte

1 sheet confectionery rice paper[+], for lining
2½ cups (375g) dried cherries[++]
⅓ cup (80ml) bourbon
¾ cup (110g) plain (all-purpose) flour, sifted
⅓ cup (35g) cocoa, sifted
2 teaspoons mixed spice
1½ cups (240g) smoked almonds, roughly chopped
120g dark (70% cocoa) chocolate, melted
¾ cup (270g) honey
1 cup (220g) white (granulated) sugar
1 vanilla bean, split and seeds scraped

Preheat oven to 160°C (325°F). Line a 20cm round springform tin with non-stick baking paper. Trim the rice paper into a round to fit the base of the tin and place it on top of the baking paper.

Place the cherries and bourbon in a medium saucepan over high heat and cook, stirring frequently, for 4–5 minutes or until the fruit is plump. Set aside to cool slightly.

Place the flour, cocoa, mixed spice, almonds, chocolate and the cherry mixture in a large bowl and mix until just combined.

Place the honey, sugar and vanilla seeds in a small saucepan over medium heat and stir until combined. Bring to the boil and cook for 2 minutes or until the temperature reaches 118°C (244°F) on a sugar (candy) thermometer. Add the honey mixture to the chocolate mixture and stir to combine.

Spoon the mixture into the tin, pressing to even the top. Bake for 40–45 minutes or until the panforte is set on the sides and slightly soft in the centre. Allow to cool in the tin for 5 hours or overnight.

Run a small knife around the edge before removing the panforte from the tin. Slice into wedges to serve. SERVES 12
+ You can find confectionery rice paper in the Asian or baking sections of the supermarket or at Asian grocers.
++ Use dried cranberries in place of cherries, if you prefer.
Tip: Keep the panforte wrapped in a cool, dark place for up to 2 weeks or refrigerated for up to 1 month. Bring to room temperature before serving.

cheat's double chocolate trifles

1½ cups (375ml) pure cream
¾ cup (185g) mascarpone
1½ tablespoons vanilla extract
12 small store-bought savoiardi (sponge finger) biscuits
chocolate dipping sauce
1 tablespoon cocoa
1 tablespoon pure maple syrup
⅓ cup (80ml) milk
chocolate ganache
120g dark (70% cocoa) chocolate, melted
½ cup (125ml) pure cream

Place the cream, mascarpone and vanilla in a large bowl and whisk until soft peaks form. Set aside.

To make the chocolate dipping sauce, place the cocoa and maple in a bowl and mix to combine. Pour in the milk and stir through. Set aside.

To make the chocolate ganache, place the melted chocolate and the cream in a small saucepan over low heat. Stir until smooth and combined. Reserve one-quarter of the chocolate ganache and set aside. Fold the remaining chocolate ganache into the whipped mascarpone mixture and gently swirl through.

To assemble, dip the sponge finger biscuits into the chocolate dipping sauce for 3 seconds and divide between serving glasses. Top with the chocolate mascarpone cream mixture and drizzle with the reserved chocolate ganache to serve. SERVES 4

cheat's double chocolate trifles

chocolate christmas pudding

chocolate christmas pudding

cup (100g) cocoa, sifted
⅔ cup (160ml) boiling water
250g unsalted butter, softened
cup (220g) caster (superfine) sugar
⅔ cup (160g) firmly packed brown sugar
2 teaspoons vanilla extract
5 eggs
cup (150g) plain (all-purpose) flour
chocolate glaze
00g dark (70% cocoa) chocolate, chopped
¼ cup (60ml) pure cream
teaspoon vanilla extract

Preheat oven to 160°C (325°F).
Place the cocoa in a heatproof bowl and gradually add the water, whisking until smooth. Set aside.
Place the butter, both the sugars and the vanilla in the bowl of an electric mixer and beat on high speed for 5 minutes or until light and creamy. Add the eggs, 1 at a time, beating well after each addition. Add the cocoa mixture and the flour and fold through until well combined (the mixture may look slightly curdled). Pour into a lightly greased 7-cup-capacity (1.75 litre) ovenproof pudding basin. Bake for 55 minutes or until cooked when tested with a skewer. Cool in the basin for 10 minutes before turning out onto a serving plate.
To make the chocolate glaze, place the chocolate, cream and vanilla in a small saucepan over low heat and stir until smooth. Allow to cool slightly before spooning over the pudding. Serve with cream or vanilla bean ice-cream. SERVES 12

espresso martini trifle

1 cup (250ml) double (thick) cream
1 tablespoon icing (confectioner's) sugar
12 store-bought almond biscotti
espresso martini jelly
¾ cup (180ml) hot espresso coffee
½ cup (120g) firmly packed brown sugar
½ cup (125ml) vodka
1 tablespoon water
1 teaspoon gelatine powder
coffee syrup
⅓ cup (80ml) hot espresso coffee
⅓ cup (80g) firmly packed brown sugar
1 tablespoon vanilla extract

To make the espresso martini jelly, place the coffee, sugar and vodka in a large heatproof jug and stir to combine. Place the water in a small bowl and sprinkle the gelatine over. Stir to dissolve. Add to the coffee mixture and stir to combine. Pour into 6 serving glasses and refrigerate for 1 hour or until set.
To make the coffee syrup, place the coffee, sugar and vanilla in a small saucepan over low heat and gently cook, stirring, for 5 minutes or until syrupy. Don't allow the mixture to boil. Set aside to cool.
Whisk the cream and icing sugar together in a bowl until soft peaks form.
To assemble, top each espresso martini jelly with 2 almond biscotti. Dollop the cream mixture over, drizzle with the coffee syrup and serve immediately. MAKES 6

Draped in a silky chocolate glaze, this dreamy pudding gives a little nod to tradition without a morsel of dried fruit in sight ... so everyone's happy!

espresso martini trifle

Beneath the *dark ripple of cocoa* that covers this tiramisu, I've snuck in *cheeky, caramelly dulce de leche* between layers of soft sponge and silky cream.

caramel brandy tiramisu

caramel brandy tiramisu

150ml egg yolk (about 9 yolks)
¾ cup (165g) caster (superfine) sugar
⅓ cup (80ml) brandy
2¼ cups (560g) mascarpone
1½ cups (375ml) pure cream
32 store-bought savoiardi (sponge finger) biscuits
1 cup (250g) store-bought good-quality dulce de leche
   (see *note*, page 129)
cocoa, for dusting
espresso soaking liquid
½ cup (125ml) brandy
1¼ cups (310ml) hot espresso coffee
¼ cup (60g) firmly packed brown sugar

Using a hand-held electric mixer, whisk the yolk, sugar and brandy in a bowl over a saucepan of gently simmering water for 8–10 minutes or until the mixture is doubled in volume. Set aside to cool slightly or continue to whisk until cooled.

In a separate bowl, use a hand-held electric mixer to whisk the mascarpone and cream together until soft peaks form. Fold the mascarpone mixture into the cooled egg mixture until combined. Set aside.

To make the espresso soaking liquid, mix the brandy, coffee and sugar in a bowl until the sugar is dissolved.

Dip the biscuits into the soaking liquid for about 3 seconds and place into a 2-litre-capacity serving dish.

Spread half the dulce de leche over the biscuits and dust with cocoa. Spoon half the mascarpone cream over the biscuits to cover. Add another layer of biscuits, spread with dulce de leche and dust with more cocoa. Finish with a layer of mascarpone cream.

Cover and refrigerate for 6–8 hours or overnight to set. Dust well with cocoa before serving. SERVES 8–10

tiramisu ice-cream cake

½ cup (110g) caster (superfine) sugar
320ml hot espresso coffee
3 litres store-bought vanilla bean ice-cream
¼ cup (60ml) brandy
18 store-bought savoiardi (sponge finger) biscuits
1 cup (250ml) double (thick) cream
½ cup (125g) mascarpone
1 teaspoon vanilla extract

Line a 10cm x 25cm loaf tin with 2 layers of non-stick baking paper, allowing the paper to extend above the rim.

Stir the sugar into the coffee until dissolved. Pour half the sweetened coffee mixture into a non-stick frying pan over low heat. Very gently cook for 10–12 minutes or until reduced to a thick syrup (for drizzling). Set aside to cool.

Place the ice-cream and the brandy in the bowl of an electric mixer and beat for 1–2 minutes or until softened and combined.

Dip the biscuits into the remaining sweetened coffee mixture for about 3 seconds, then place 6 of the soaked biscuits into the prepared tin. Top with one-third of the ice-cream mixture. Continue layering with the soaked biscuits and ice-cream mixture, finishing with a layer of the ice-cream mixture. Cover and freeze for at least 6 hours or overnight.

Place the cream, mascarpone and vanilla in a bowl and whisk until soft peaks form.

Invert the frozen tiramisu onto a serving dish. Cover the tin with a warm cloth and use the overhanging paper to carefully remove the cake from the tin. Remove the paper and discard. Dollop with the cream mixture, drizzle with the coffee syrup and serve immediately. **SERVES 8-10**
Tip: Do not allow the coffee syrup to boil or it will become bitter.

tiramisu ice-cream cake

fig and date ice-cream cake with brandy syrup

fig and date ice-cream cake with brandy syrup

3 soft fresh dates (60g), pitted and roughly chopped
¼ cup (50g) dried figs, roughly chopped
½ teaspoon bicarbonate of (baking) soda
⅓ cup (80ml) boiling water
60g unsalted butter, softened
½ teaspoon vanilla extract
½ cup (120g) firmly packed brown sugar
2 eggs
⅔ cup (100g) self-raising (self-rising) flour, sifted
¼ cup (30g) almond meal (ground almonds)
1½ tablespoons golden syrup
¼ cup (35g) slivered pistachios
2 litres store-bought vanilla bean ice-cream
brandy syrup
1 cup (220g) caster (superfine) sugar
1 cup (250ml) brandy
½ cup (125ml) water
1 cup (180g) semi-dried baby figs

To make the brandy syrup, place the sugar, brandy and water in a medium saucepan over low heat and cook, stirring, until the sugar is dissolved. Increase the heat to high, bring to the boil and cook for 8–10 minutes or until syrupy. Add the baby figs and set aside to cool completely.

Place the dates, dried figs, bicarbonate of soda and water in a small bowl. Allow to soak for 15 minutes. Place in a food processor and process until smooth.

Preheat oven to 160°C (325°F). Line a deep 20cm round springform tin with non-stick baking paper.

Place the butter, vanilla and sugar in the bowl of an electric mixer and beat for 2–3 minutes or until pale and creamy. Add the eggs, 1 at a time, beating well after each addition. Add the flour, date mixture, almond meal, golden syrup and pistachios and beat to combine. Spoon into the tin and bake for 40–45 minutes or until cooked when tested with a skewer. Allow the cake to cool in the tin for 10 minutes. Turn out onto a wire rack to cool completely.

Re-line the cleaned tin. Scoop the ice-cream into the clean bowl of an electric mixer and beat on low speed until softened. Spoon the ice-cream into the tin and smooth the top. Freeze for 3–4 hours or until set. Remove the ice-cream from the tin. Place on a cake stand or plate and top with the cooled cake. Spoon the brandy syrup over and slice to serve. SERVES 8

raspberry, white chocolate and pistachio ice-cream cake

1½ cups (375ml) strained raspberry puree[+]
½ cup (110g) caster (superfine) sugar
2 tablespoons lemon juice
125g raspberries
¼ cup (35g) shelled unsalted pistachios, halved
icing (confectioner's) sugar, for dusting
white chocolate ice-cream
200g white chocolate, chopped
2 cups (500ml) pure cream
3 eggs, plus 2 egg yolks extra
1 teaspoon vanilla extract
½ cup (110g) caster (superfine) sugar
½ cup (125ml) coconut cream

Line a 8cm x 32cm loaf tin with 2 layers of non-stick baking paper. Place the raspberry puree, sugar and lemon juice in a large bowl and stir until the sugar is dissolved. Pour into the base of the prepared tin. Freeze for 2 hours or until set.

To make the white chocolate ice-cream, place the white chocolate and ½ cup (125ml) of the cream in a heatproof bowl over a saucepan of simmering water (the bowl shouldn't touch the water) and stir until melted and smooth. Set aside.

Place the eggs, extra yolks, vanilla and sugar in a heatproof bowl over a saucepan of simmering water and, using a hand-held electric mixer, whisk for 6–8 minutes or until thick and pale. Remove from the heat and whisk for a further 6–8 minutes or until cool. Gently fold through the melted white chocolate mixture and set aside.

Whisk the remaining 1½ cups (375ml) cream and coconut cream together until soft peaks form. Add the egg mixture and gently fold through until well combined. Pour over the raspberry layer. Cover with foil and freeze overnight.

Invert the ice-cream cake onto a serving plate and remove the baking paper. Scatter the raspberries over the top and sprinkle with the pistachios. Dust with icing sugar, cut into slices and serve immediately. SERVES 12–14

+ *To make 1½ cups of raspberry puree, you will need to blend 6 cups (750g) thawed frozen raspberries until smooth. Press through a fine sieve and discard the seeds.*

This is the ultimate *make-ahead dessert*. Decadently creamy white chocolate ice-cream topped with *tangy raspberry sorbet*. Scatter with berries, pistachios and a *delicate snowfall of sugar* for the ta-dah! moment.

raspberry, white chocolate and pistachio ice-cream cake

raspberry and white chocolate trifle

raspberry and white chocolate trifle

½ cup (125ml) orange liqueur
20 small store-bought savoiardi (sponge finger) biscuits
  (see *cook's tips*, page 178)
250g fresh raspberries, to serve
raspberry jelly
1.5 litres cranberry juice
2 tablespoons gelatine powder
1 cup (220g) caster (superfine) sugar
3¾ cups (470g) frozen raspberries
white chocolate ganache
180g white chocolate, finely chopped
1 cup (250ml) pure cream
mascarpone cream
½ cup (125g) mascarpone
½ cup (80g) icing (confectioner's) sugar, sifted
1 teaspoon vanilla bean paste or vanilla extract
1½ cups (375ml) pure cream

To make the raspberry jelly, place 1 cup (250ml) of the cranberry juice in a small bowl. Slowly sprinkle with the gelatine and set aside for 5 minutes or until the gelatine is absorbed. Place the remaining juice and the sugar in a large saucepan over medium heat and stir until the sugar is dissolved. Bring to the boil and cook for 1 minute. Remove from the heat, add the gelatine mixture and whisk to combine. Allow to stand for 20 minutes or until cool. Pour into a 4-litre-capacity glass dish and top with the frozen raspberries. Refrigerate for 4–5 hours or overnight until set (see *cook's tips*, page 178).

To make the white chocolate ganache, place the chocolate in a small saucepan over low heat and stir until melted and smooth. Remove from the heat and add ¼ cup (60ml) of the cream in a thin, steady stream, stirring constantly until well combined. Allow to cool slightly and refrigerate until just cold. Place the remaining ¾ cup (180ml) of cream in the bowl of an electric mixer and whisk on high speed until stiff peaks form. Add the cooled chocolate mixture and gently fold to combine.

To make the mascarpone cream, place the mascarpone, sugar, vanilla and cream in the clean bowl of an electric mixer and whisk until soft peaks form.

To assemble the trifle, spoon the ganache over the jelly and smooth the top, using a palette knife. Place the liqueur in a small shallow bowl. Dip the biscuits in the liqueur and layer them over the ganache. Spoon the mascarpone cream over the biscuits and sprinkle with the fresh raspberries to serve. SERVES 6-8

first make the jelly

then whip up the ganache

spoon it onto the set base

spread until smooth

arrange the biscuits

top with cream and berries

cook's tips

○ You can make the raspberry jelly 1–2 days in advance, before proceeding with the ganache, sponge and mascarpone cream layers.

○ Don't hesitate to mix up the flavours in your trifle. Use frozen cherries in the jelly and fresh cherries on top, or try swapping in blueberries or strawberries.

○ Depending on the size of the sponge finger biscuits and your glass trifle bowl, you may need to trim the biscuits to fit.

○ The trick to creating a show-stopping trifle is to keep the layers visible through the glass dish. Try to smooth the ganache as neatly as you can and layer the sponge fingers in a pretty pattern.

○ Using frozen berries in the jelly layer of the trifle helps to cool and set the mixture.

fig and caramel trifle

fig and caramel trifle

1 x 1kg store-bought panettone, ends trimmed and
  cut into 2.5cm-thick slices
⅓ cup (80ml) Pedro Ximénez sherry or fresh orange juice
2 cups (500g) mascarpone
2⅓ cups (580ml) double (thick) cream
caramel
100g unsalted butter, chopped
¾ cup (180g) firmly packed dark brown sugar
½ cup (175g) golden syrup
1 cup (250ml) pure cream
caramelised figs
¼ cup (55g) raw caster (superfine) sugar
1 tablespoon coffee sugar crystals[+]
6 figs, halved lengthways

To make the caramel, place the butter, brown sugar, golden syrup and pure cream in a medium saucepan over medium heat. Stir until the sugar is dissolved. Bring to the boil and cook, stirring occasionally, for 10–12 minutes or until thickened. Allow to cool.

To make the caramelised figs, place the raw sugar and coffee sugar crystals in a bowl and stir to combine. Heat a non-stick frying pan over high heat. Dip the cut-side of the figs in the sugar to coat them. Add the figs, cut-side down, to the pan and cook for 10–20 seconds or until caramelised. Remove from the pan and allow to stand until the sugar is set.

Preheat oven grill (broiler) to medium heat.

Brush both sides of the panettone slices with the sherry or juice. Place on a baking tray and grill, in batches, for 30 seconds each side or until golden. Cut each panettone slice into 3 strips.

Place the mascarpone and double cream in the bowl of an electric mixer and whisk on high speed until stiff peaks form.

To assemble, line the base of a 4-litre-capacity glass dish with half the panettone. Spoon half the mascarpone cream mixture over the top and follow with half the caramel. Repeat the layers once more with the remaining panettone, mascarpone cream mixture and caramel. Top with the caramelised figs to serve. SERVES 12–14

+ *Coffee sugar crystals have a full-bodied caramel flavour and a deep honey colour. Find them at most supermarkets or at specialty stores.*

What's Christmas without a towering trifle (or two)? *Rich and glossy caramel* peeks through layers of sherry-soaked panettone and mascarpone cream, with a *crown of sticky figs shimmering on top.*

lemon meringue trifle

1½ cups (525g) store-bought lemon curd
lemon yoghurt cake
¾ cup (180ml) light-flavoured extra virgin olive oil
2 eggs
1 tablespoon finely grated lemon rind
¼ cup (60ml) lemon juice
1 cup (280g) plain thick yoghurt
1¾ cups (385g) caster (superfine) sugar
2 cups (300g) self-raising (self-rising) flour
lemon and tonic syrup
¼ cup (55g) caster (superfine) sugar
½ cup (125ml) tonic water
1 tablespoon lemon juice
¼ cup (60ml) gin (optional)
whipped cream
600ml double (thick) cream
600ml pure cream
2 tablespoons pure icing (confectioner's) sugar
Italian meringue
⅓ cup (80ml) water
½ teaspoon cream of tartar
2 cups (440g) caster (superfine) sugar
150ml eggwhite (about 4 eggs), at room temperature
   (see *cook's tips*, page 151)

Preheat oven to 160°C (325°F). Line a 20cm x 30cm slice tin with non-stick baking paper.

To make the lemon yoghurt cake, place the oil, eggs, lemon rind and juice, yoghurt and sugar in a large bowl and whisk to combine. Sift in the flour and whisk until smooth.

Pour into the prepared tin and bake for 35–40 minutes or until cooked through when tested with a skewer. Cool in the tin for 5 minutes, before turning out onto a wire rack to cool completely. Cut the cake into 5cm x 7cm rectangles and set aside.

To make the lemon and tonic syrup, place the sugar, tonic water and lemon juice in a small saucepan over medium heat and stir until the sugar is dissolved. Cook for 2 minutes or until thickened slightly. Remove from the heat. Stir in the gin, if desired. Set aside to cool.

To make the whipped cream, place both the creams and the icing sugar in the bowl of an electric mixer and whisk until soft peaks form. Set aside.

To make the Italian meringue, place the water, cream of tartar and 1 cup (220g) of the sugar in a small saucepan over high heat. Cook, stirring, until the sugar is dissolved. Bring to the boil, reduce the heat to a simmer and cook for 4 minutes.

Place the eggwhite in the clean bowl of an electric mixer and whisk on high speed until stiff peaks form. With the motor running, gradually add the remaining sugar, 1 tablespoon at a time, whisking for 30 seconds before adding more. Gradually add the hot sugar syrup in a thin, steady stream and whisk for a further 4 minutes or until the meringue is thick, glossy and cooled.

To assemble, place the lemon yoghurt cake pieces in the base of a 4-litre-capacity glass dish and drizzle with the lemon and tonic syrup. Spoon over the whipped cream and top with the lemon curd. Dollop the Italian meringue on top and use a small kitchen blowtorch to lightly toast the meringue until golden brown. Serve immediately.
SERVES 6-8

Your *favourite tart* but in a zesty trifle! With its *light and lemony* yoghurt cake base, ginny syrup, billows of cream and scorched meringue topping, this *sunset-soaked stunner* epitomises festive feasting.

lemon meringue trifle

gingerbread, sherry and caramel trifle

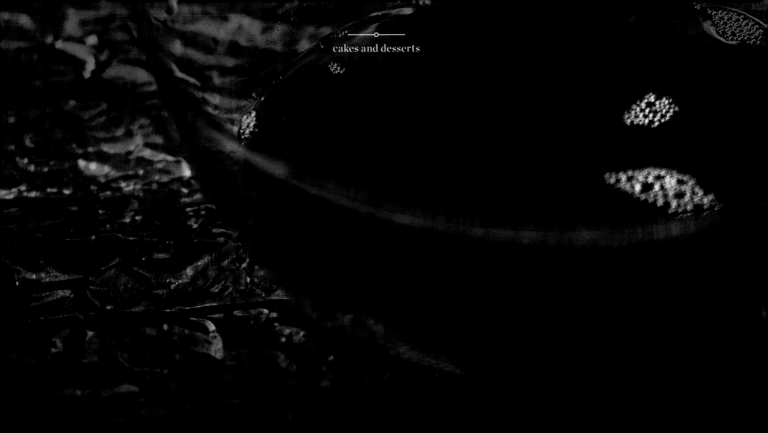

gingerbread, sherry and caramel trifle

3 cups (750ml) pure cream
3 cups (720g) sour cream
½ cup (150g) store-bought good-quality dulce de leche
 (see *note*, page 129)
gingerbread cake
1⅔ cups (250g) plain (all-purpose) flour, sifted
2½ teaspoons baking powder, sifted
2 teaspoons ground ginger
1 teaspoon mixed spice
1 cup (240g) firmly packed dark brown sugar
125g unsalted butter, chopped
½ cup (175g) golden syrup
½ cup (180g) honey
1 egg, lightly whisked
1¼ cups (310ml) milk
Pedro Ximénez jelly
3 cups (750ml) water
1½ tablespoons gelatine powder
1 cup (250ml) Pedro Ximénez sherry
1 cup (220g) caster (superfine) sugar

To make the gingerbread cake, preheat oven to 180°C
(350°F). Line a 24cm round tin with non-stick baking paper.
 Place the flour, baking powder, ginger, mixed spice and
sugar in a large bowl and mix to combine.

Place the butter, golden syrup and honey in a small
saucepan over low heat and stir until melted and smooth.
Add the butter mixture, the egg and milk to the flour
mixture and whisk until smooth. Pour into the tin and
bake for 1 hour or until cooked when tested with a skewer.
Turn out onto a wire rack and allow to cool completely.
 To make the Pedro Ximénez jelly, place ½ cup (125ml)
of the water in a small bowl. Slowly sprinkle with the gelatine
and set aside for 5 minutes or until the gelatine is absorbed.
Place the remaining 2½ cups (625ml) of water, the sherry
and sugar in a medium saucepan over medium heat and stir
until the sugar is dissolved. Bring to the boil and cook for
1 minute. Remove from the heat, add the gelatine mixture
and whisk to combine. Allow to stand for 15 minutes or until
cool. Pour into a 4-litre-capacity glass dish. Refrigerate for
2 hours or until set.
 To assemble the trifle, place the cream and sour cream in
the bowl of an electric mixer and whisk until soft peaks form.
Using a large serrated knife, cut the cooled cake in half
horizontally. Trim the cake layers to fit the glass dish. Place
half the cake on top of the jelly. Spoon one-third of the
cream mixture onto the cake and smooth with a palette knife.
Top with the remaining cake and cream mixture. Spoon the
dulce de leche on top and fold into the cream to create a
swirled effect. Refrigerate until ready to serve. **SERVES 12-14**
*Tip: You can make the gingerbread cake 1–2 days ahead. The
trifle can be assembled up to 2–3 hours in advance.*

chocolate and cherry cranberry jelly trifle

1 cup (350g) store-bought cherry jam
fresh cherries, to serve
cherry cranberry jelly
3 cups (750ml) cranberry juice
1 tablespoon gelatine powder
½ cup (110g) caster (superfine) sugar
3¾ cups (560g) frozen pitted cherries
fudgy chocolate cake
250g unsalted butter, chopped
300g dark (70% cocoa) chocolate, chopped
2 tablespoons cocoa, sifted
½ cup (125ml) milk
6 eggs
1 cup (220g) caster (superfine) sugar
½ cup (120g) firmly packed brown sugar
1 cup (150g) plain (all-purpose) flour
mascarpone and chocolate cream
600ml pure cream
1 cup (250g) mascarpone
¼ cup (40g) icing (confectioner's) sugar, sifted
100g dark (70% cocoa) chocolate, extra,
—shaved using a vegetable peeler

To make the cherry cranberry jelly, place 1 cup (250ml) of the cranberry juice in a small bowl. Slowly sprinkle with the gelatine and allow to stand for 5 minutes or until the gelatine is absorbed. Place the remaining 2 cups (500ml) juice and the sugar in a large saucepan over medium heat and stir until the sugar is dissolved. Bring to the boil and cook for 1 minute. Remove from the heat, add the gelatine mixture and gently whisk to combine. Strain the cranberry mixture and pour into a 4-litre-capacity glass dish. Allow to stand for 20 minutes or until cool. Top with the frozen cherries. Refrigerate for 4–5 hours or overnight to set.

Preheat oven to 160°C (325°F). Line a 22cm round cake tin with non-stick baking paper.

To make the fudgy chocolate cake, place the butter and the chopped chocolate in a medium saucepan over low heat and stir until melted and smooth. Add the cocoa and milk and stir to combine. Set aside to cool slightly.

Place the eggs and both the sugars in the bowl of an electric mixer and whisk on high speed for 12–15 minutes or until pale, thick and creamy.

Add the chocolate mixture to the egg mixture and whisk, scraping down the sides of the bowl, until just combined. Reduce the speed to low, add the flour and whisk until just combined.

Pour the cake mixture into the prepared tin and bake for 1 hour–1 hour 10 minutes or until just set+. Allow to cool completely in the tin.

To make the mascarpone and chocolate cream, place the cream, mascarpone and icing sugar in the clean bowl of an electric mixer and whisk until soft peaks form. Add half the extra shaved chocolate and gently fold through.

To assemble the trifle, place the chocolate cake over the jelly. Spoon the cherry jam onto the chocolate cake and top with the mascarpone and chocolate cream. Sprinkle with the remaining shaved chocolate and finish with fresh cherries. SERVES 6–8

+ *The cake is ready when it feels set to the touch. If tested, a skewer won't come out clean – the cake will set with a fudgy centre as it cools.*

chocolate and cherry cranberry jelly trifle

cookies and treats

The best gifts are the ones you can eat! These *made-with-love* morsels will satisfy sweet tooths with their irresistible *snap, crackle and crunch* – including everyone's favourite salty-meets-sweet treat – a *rocking rocky road.*

choc-caramel coconut bars

choc-caramel coconut bars

300g dark (70% cocoa) chocolate, chopped
biscuit base
1 cup (80g) desiccated coconut
½ cup (60g) almond meal (ground almonds)
⅓ cup (80ml) pure maple syrup
2 tablespoons light-flavoured extra virgin olive oil
caramel filling
½ cup (125ml) coconut cream
¾ cup (180ml) pure maple syrup
½ teaspoon sea salt flakes, plus extra to serve
⅓ cup (80g) cashew butter
2 teaspoons vanilla extract

Preheat oven to 160°C (325°F). Line a 20cm square cake tin with 2 layers of non-stick baking paper.

To make the biscuit base, combine the coconut, almond meal, maple and oil. Press the mixture into the tin and bake for 25–30 minutes or until crisp and golden. Allow to cool.

To make the caramel filling, place the coconut cream, maple and salt in a frying pan over high heat. Bring to the boil and cook for 10 minutes, stirring occasionally, until thickened. Add the cashew butter and vanilla, reduce the heat to medium and cook, stirring constantly, for 2 minutes.

Pour the caramel filling over the biscuit base and refrigerate for 30 minutes or until set. Cut into 12 bars.

Melt the chocolate in a small saucepan over medium heat. Allow to cool for 10 minutes. Using 2 forks, dip each bar in the melted chocolate and tap off the excess. Place on a baking tray lined with non-stick baking paper. Sprinkle with the extra salt and refrigerate for 30 minutes or until set. MAKES 12 BARS
Tips: These bars will keep in an airtight container in the refrigerator for up to 2 weeks. Wrap in non-stick baking paper and tie with ribbon to make sweet edible gifts.

chocolate caramel brittle

450g unsalted butter, chopped
2 cups (440g) white (granulated) sugar
2 tablespoons glucose syrup
½ cup (125ml) water
300g dark (70% cocoa) chocolate, finely chopped

Line a 24cm x 34cm baking tray with non-stick baking paper.

Place the butter in a saucepan over medium heat.

Stir until melted. Add the sugar, glucose syrup and water and stir with a metal spoon to combine. Place a sugar (candy) thermometer into the sugar mixture and cook for 22–25 minutes, stirring occasionally when the sugar thermometer reads above 140°C (284°F). When the sugar thermometer reaches 152°C, remove from the heat and, working quickly, pour the caramel onto the tray and allow to stand for 5 minutes.

Sprinkle the chocolate over the caramel and let it melt for 2 minutes. Using a palette knife, smooth the chocolate. Allow to stand at room temperature for 10 minutes, then refrigerate for 40 minutes or until set.

Break the brittle into shards to serve. SERVES 10–12
Tip: Store the brittle in an airtight container for up to 1 week.

carrot cake granola

4 cups (360g) rolled oats
2 cups (240g) grated carrot
2 cups (230g) roughly chopped pecans
2 cups (200g) roughly chopped walnuts
1 cup (75g) shredded coconut
3 teaspoons ground cinnamon
1½ teaspoons ground ginger
1½ teaspoons ground nutmeg
1 cup (250ml) pure maple syrup
½ cup (125ml) light-flavoured extra virgin olive oil
1 tablespoon vanilla extract
1⅓ cups (220g) raisins[+]

Preheat oven to 160°C (325°F). Line 3 large baking trays with non-stick baking paper.

Place the oats, carrot, pecans, walnuts, coconut, cinnamon, ginger and nutmeg in a large bowl and mix to combine. Add the maple syrup, oil and vanilla and gently mix to coat.

Divide the mixture between the prepared trays, spreading it out evenly. Bake for 20 minutes. Stir the mixture and bake for a further 10–15 minutes or until the granola is golden and crunchy. Allow to cool on the trays. Add the raisins and toss through to serve. MAKES 12 CUPS
+ You can use dried cranberries instead of raisin.
Tips: The granola will keep in an airtight container for up to 4 weeks.

If you're gifting this granola, store in glass jars, cover with a lid and decorate with a piece of calico that is tied with natural jute ribbon or string. For a decorative touch, add a sprig of maple leaves or any other foliage that you have in your garden.

carrot cake granola

chocolate caramel brittle

raspberry and vanilla coconut ice

raspberry and vanilla coconut ice

1.28kg icing (confectioner's) sugar, sifted
6 cups (480g) desiccated coconut
½ teaspoon vanilla extract
1½ cups (375ml) sweetened condensed milk
plain (all-purpose) flour, for dusting
1 cup (125g) frozen raspberries, thawed
1–2 drops red food colouring

Line a 20cm x 30cm slice tin with non-stick baking paper. Place 4 cups (640g) of the sugar, 3 cups (240g) of the coconut and the vanilla in a large bowl. Add 1¼ cups (310ml) of the sweetened condensed milk and mix well to combine. Turn the mixture out onto a lightly floured surface and knead until smooth. Press evenly into the base of the tin and set aside.

Place the remaining 4 cups (640g) of sugar and 3 cups (240g) of coconut in a large bowl. Add the raspberries and food colouring and, using your fingers, rub the mixture until the raspberries are well combined. Add the remaining ¼ cup (65ml) of condensed milk and mix to combine. Turn the mixture out onto a lightly floured surface and knead until smooth. Press the raspberry mixture into the tin over the vanilla layer. Cover and refrigerate for 3–4 hours or until set.

Slice the coconut ice into pieces to serve. MAKES 50
Tip: Store coconut ice in an airtight container in the refrigerator for up to 2 weeks. Bring to room temperature before serving.

chocolate pecan pie bars

200g dark (70% cocoa) chocolate, chopped
80g unsalted butter
1 cup (240g) firmly packed brown sugar
1 cup (350g) golden syrup
½ cup (125ml) pure cream
7 eggs
1 cup (200g) chopped candied clementines+
3 cups (360g) pecans, roughly chopped
chocolate pastry
¼ cup (25g) cocoa
1½ cups (225g) plain (all-purpose) flour
125g cold unsalted butter, chopped
½ cup (80g) icing (confectioner's) sugar
3 egg yolks
1 tablespoon iced water
1 eggwhite, lightly whisked

To make the chocolate pastry, line a 30cm x 40cm Swiss roll tin with non-stick baking paper. Place the cocoa, flour, butter and icing sugar in a food processor and process until the mixture resembles fine breadcrumbs. With the motor running, add the egg yolks and process to combine. Add the water and process until a dough comes together. Turn the dough out and press it into the base of the tin. Smooth the top with the back of a spoon, brush with the eggwhite and refrigerate for 20 minutes or until firm.

Preheat oven to 160°C (325°F).

Place the chocolate and butter in a heatproof bowl over a saucepan of simmering water (the bowl shouldn't touch the water) and stir until melted and smooth. Allow to cool slightly.

Place the brown sugar, golden syrup, cream and eggs in a large bowl. Add the chocolate mixture and whisk until well combined. Add the clementines and mix to combine. Spoon the mixture over the pastry, spread evenly and decorate with the pecans. Bake for 40–45 minutes or until just set. Allow to cool in the tin for 20 minutes, then refrigerate until cold.

Remove the slice from the tin, trim the edges and cut into bars to serve. MAKES 30
+ Candied clementines are available from specialty food stores.
Tip: Store the bars in an airtight container in the refrigerator for up to 3–4 days.

chocolate pecan pie bars

rocky road

rocky road

1kg dark (70% cocoa) chocolate, chopped
2 tablespoons vegetable oil
1 cup (140g) dried cranberries
200g store-bought marshmallows
250g store-bought Turkish delight pieces
1 cup (50g) coconut flakes
1 cup (140g) shelled unsalted pistachios, chopped

Line a 25cm x 32cm slice tin with non-stick baking paper.
Place the chocolate and oil in a large heatproof bowl
over a saucepan of simmering water (the bowl shouldn't
touch the water) and stir until melted and smooth.
 Place the cranberries, marshmallows, Turkish delight,
coconut and pistachios in a large bowl and mix to combine.
Reserve and set aside 1 cup (250ml) of the melted
chocolate. Add the remaining chocolate to the rocky road
mixture and stir to combine. Spoon the mixture into the tin,
pressing down gently to spread it to the edges. Pour the
reserved chocolate over the rocky road and spread evenly
with a palette knife. Refrigerate for 30 minutes or until set.
 Remove the rocky road from the tin and slice into long
bars to serve. MAKES 6
Tips: Store the rocky road in a cool, dry place for up to 1 week.
Wrap bars in paper and tie with ribbon to make sweet edible gifts.

chewy caramels with salted peanuts

3 cups (420g) salted peanuts
1.1kg white (granulated) sugar
1.125 litres pure cream
1 cup (350g) golden syrup
100g unsalted butter, chopped

Line a 20cm x 30cm slice tin with non-stick baking paper[+].
Sprinkle the base with 1½ cups (210g) of the peanuts and
set aside.
 Place the sugar, cream, golden syrup and butter in a
large saucepan over high heat and stir with a metal spoon
until the butter and sugar have melted. Reduce the heat
to medium and cook, stirring, for 20–25 minutes or until
the temperature reaches 122°C (251°F) on a sugar (candy)
thermometer. Working quickly, pour the caramel into the
tin and carefully sprinkle with the remaining 1½ cups (210g)
of peanuts. Allow to cool completely at room temperature
for 3–4 hours. Refrigerate for 25–30 minutes or until firm.
 Turn the caramel out onto a board and, using a large
sharp knife, cut into pieces[++]. Wrap each caramel in brown
wax paper, twisting the ends to seal. Keep refrigerated and
bring to room temperature to serve. MAKES 50
+ It's best to work quickly but carefully when making caramel
– line your tin and measure the ingredients before you begin.
++ If the caramel becomes too soft to cut, simply return it to
the refrigerator for 5 minutes.
Tip: Store the caramels, wrapped in non-stick baking paper,
in the refrigerator for up to 2 weeks.

chewy caramels with salted peanuts

almond, cranberry and nougat bark

400g dark (70% cocoa) chocolate, melted
⅓ cup (55g) almonds, toasted and chopped
½ cup (70g) dried cranberries
150g store-bought almond nougat, chopped

Line a large baking tray with non-stick baking paper. Pour 350g of the melted chocolate onto the tray and, using a palette knife, spread into a thin layer. Sprinkle with the chopped almonds, the cranberries and nougat. Refrigerate for 1 hour or until set.

Using a teaspoon, drizzle with the remaining 50g melted chocolate and refrigerate for 10 minutes or until set.

Break the bark into pieces to serve. SERVES 8

Tip: Store the bark in an airtight container in the refrigerator for up to 3 days.

frozen coconut and nougat slice

2 litres store-bought vanilla bean ice-cream, softened
1½ cups (50g) puffed brown rice
1½ cups (110g) shredded coconut, plus extra to serve
200g store-bought almond nougat, finely chopped

Line a 20cm x 30cm slice tin with non-stick baking paper. Place the ice-cream, puffed rice, coconut and nougat in a large bowl and, working quickly, mix to combine. Spoon into the tin and smooth the top with a palette knife. Freeze for 3–4 hours or until firm.

Remove the slice from the tin and cut into squares. Sprinkle with the extra coconut to serve. MAKES 20

nougat, ginger and mascarpone trifles

¾ cup (185g) mascarpone
1¼ cups (310ml) pure cream
1 teaspoon vanilla extract
200g store-bought almond nougat, thinly sliced
    using a serrated knife
¼ cup (55g) crystallised ginger, finely chopped
store-bought ginger syrup, to serve⁺

Place the mascarpone, cream and vanilla in a medium bowl
and whisk until soft peaks form.
   Divide the mascarpone mixture, nougat and crystallised
ginger between serving glasses to create a layered effect.
   Drizzle the trifles with ginger syrup to serve. MAKES 4
+ You can find ginger syrup at specialty grocers or
delicatessens. If unavailable, use honey in its place.

chocolate and raspberry dipped nougat

100g dark (70% cocoa) chocolate, melted
½ teaspoon vegetable oil
300g store-bought almond nougat, cut into 2cm pieces
1 tablespoon freeze-dried raspberries⁺, crushed

Line a small baking tray with non-stick baking paper. Place
the chocolate and oil in a small bowl and mix to combine.
   Dip 1 end of each nougat piece into the chocolate
mixture, shaking off any excess, and place on the tray.
Sprinkle with the freeze-dried raspberries and refrigerate
for 15 minutes or until set, before serving. MAKES 10
+ Freeze-dried raspberries are available from select delicatessens
and specialty grocers.
Tip: Store the nougat in an airtight container for up to 3 days.

caramel swirl marshmallows

caramel swirl marshmallows

½ cup (125ml) warm water
2 tablespoons gelatine powder
1½ cups (330g) caster (superfine) sugar
⅔ cup (230g) liquid glucose
½ cup (125ml) water, extra
½ cup (150g) store-bought good-quality dulce de leche
    (see *note*, page 129)
1 cup (160g) icing (confectioner's) sugar, sifted, plus extra
    for dusting

Line a 20cm x 30cm slice tin with non-stick baking paper, allowing 3cm of paper to extend above the edges. Place the warm water in the bowl of an electric mixer and slowly sprinkle with the gelatine. Set aside for 5 minutes or until the gelatine is absorbed.

Place the caster sugar, glucose and the extra water in a medium saucepan over low heat. Cook, stirring, until the sugar is dissolved. Increase the heat to high and bring to the boil. Cook, without stirring, for 6–7 minutes or until the temperature reaches 115°C (239°F) on a sugar (candy) thermometer.

With the electric mixer on high speed, gradually add the hot syrup to the gelatine mixture in a thin steady stream and whisk for 3 minutes or until thick and glossy. Working quickly, add the dulce de leche and gently fold to combine. Carefully spoon the mixture into the tin. Use a sheet of non-stick baking paper to help you carefully smooth the marshmallow into an even layer. Refrigerate for 1–2 hours or until set.

Use the paper to help you lift the marshmallow from the tin. Dust a large knife with extra icing sugar. Trim the edges and cut the marshmallow into squares. Dust the squares with the icing sugar to serve. MAKES 15
Tip: Store these marshmallows in an airtight container in the refrigerator for up to 1 week.

twisted honey caramels

1 cup (250ml) double (thick) cream
65g unsalted butter, chopped
1⅓ cups (295g) white (granulated) sugar
⅔ cup (240g) honey
sea salt flakes (optional), to serve

Line a 20cm square cake tin with non-stick baking paper[+]. Place the cream and butter in a small saucepan over low heat and stir until the butter is melted. Set aside and keep warm.

Place the sugar and honey in a medium deep-sided saucepan over medium heat and cook, stirring occasionally, until the sugar is dissolved. Bring to the boil and cook, brushing any sugar crystals down the sides of the pan with a wet pastry brush, for 6–7 minutes or until the temperature reaches 154°C (309°F) on a sugar (candy) thermometer. Gradually add the warm cream mixture and mix well to combine[++]. Cook for a further 11–12 minutes or until the temperature reaches 127°C (260°F).

Working quickly, carefully pour the caramel into the tin and allow to stand at room temperature for 4 hours or until firm.

Slice the caramel into 1cm-wide lengths, halve each length and twist the caramels from each end. Wrap in squares of non-stick baking paper and twist the ends to seal. Refrigerate until needed. Sprinkle with sea salt to serve. MAKES 40
+ *It's best to work quickly but carefully when making caramel – line your tin and measure the ingredients before you begin.*
++ *When pouring the cream into the syrup, the hot mixture will boil and bubble – take care and use a deep saucepan.*
Tip: Store these caramels in the refrigerator for up to 1 week.

twisted honey caramels

black sea salt and chocolate caramel macarons

salted caramel doughnuts

¾ cup (180ml) lukewarm milk
3 teaspoons dry yeast
¾ cup (165g) raw caster (superfine) sugar
2 cups (300g) plain (all-purpose) flour,
    plus extra for dusting
2 egg yolks
50g unsalted butter, softened
1 teaspoon ground cinnamon
vegetable oil, for deep-frying
salted caramel filling
¾ cup (225g) store-bought good-quality dulce de leche
    (see *note*, page 129)
¾ cup (185g) mascarpone
sea salt flakes

Combine the milk, yeast and 1 tablespoon of the sugar in a
small jug. Allow to stand in a warm place for 5–10 minutes
or until the surface is foamy.

Place the flour, egg yolks, butter, yeast mixture and
2 tablespoons of the sugar in the bowl of an electric mixer
with the dough hook attached. Beat on low speed for
4–5 minutes or until the dough is smooth and elastic.
Place in a lightly greased bowl, cover and allow to stand
in a warm place for 45 minutes or until doubled in size.

Line a large baking tray with non-stick baking paper.
Turn the dough out onto a lightly floured surface and
knead for 2 minutes or until smooth and elastic. Roll out
to 1cm thick. Using a 5.5cm round cutter lightly dusted in
flour, cut 20 rounds from the dough. Place the rounds on
the tray and cover loosely. Allow to stand in a warm place
for 25–30 minutes or until doubled in size.

While the dough is proving, make the salted caramel
filling. Whisk the dulce de leche, mascarpone and a pinch
of salt together until smooth. Place in a piping bag fitted
with a 5mm round nozzle and refrigerate until needed.

Combine the remaining ½ cup (110g) sugar and the
cinnamon in a shallow bowl and set aside. Half-fill a large
deep saucepan with oil and place over medium heat, until
the temperature reaches 160°C (325°F) on a deep-frying
thermometer. Cook the dough rounds, in batches, turning
halfway, for 1–2 minutes or until golden. Toss in the
cinnamon sugar. Using a small sharp knife, cut a hole in
the side of each doughnut and pipe the salted caramel
filling in to serve. MAKES 20

black sea salt and chocolate caramel macarons

1¼ cups (200g) pure icing (confectioner's) sugar
¾ cup (90g) almond meal (ground almonds)
¼ cup (25g) cocoa
3 eggwhites (see *cook's tips*, page 151), at room temperature
1 tablespoon caster (superfine) sugar
2 teaspoons black sea salt flakes (see *note*, page 72)
1 cup (300g) good-quality store-bought dulce de leche
    (see *note*, page 129)

Preheat oven to 150°C (300°F). Line 2 large baking trays
with non-stick baking paper.

Sift the icing sugar, almond meal and cocoa into a large
bowl. Mix to combine and set aside.

Place the eggwhites in the bowl of an electric mixer and
whisk on high speed for 30 seconds. Add the caster sugar and
whisk for 10 minutes or until stiff peaks form and the sugar
is dissolved. In 2 batches, add the cocoa mixture and gently
fold to combine. Spoon the mixture into a piping bag fitted
with a 1.5cm round nozzle and pipe 32 x 4cm rounds onto
the trays. Gently tap the trays on a benchtop to remove
any air bubbles and allow to stand for 30 minutes or until
a skin forms on the surface of the macarons.

Sprinkle half the macarons with the salt. Reduce the
oven temperature to 130°C (260°F) and bake for
15–18 minutes or until crisp on the outside and chewy
in the centre. Allow to cool completely on the trays.

Spoon the dulce de leche onto the underside of the
unsalted macarons and sandwich with the remaining
macarons to serve. MAKES 16

*Tip: These macarons will keep, unfilled, in an airtight container
for 1–2 days. Fill them on the day you plan to serve them.*

salted caramel doughnuts

fruit mince pies

fruit mince pies

1 Granny Smith (green) apple, peeled and grated

⅔ cup (110g) dried currants

¾ cup (120g) sultanas

½ cup (70g) slivered almonds

⅔ cup (110g) mixed peel

⅓ cup (80ml) pure maple syrup

½ cup (120g) firmly packed brown sugar

60g unsalted butter, chopped

⅓ cup (80ml) butterscotch schnapps or sherry

1 egg, lightly whisked

white (granulated) sugar, for sprinkling
    (see *cook's tips*, page 210)

icing (confectioner's) sugar, for dusting

spiced brown sugar pastry

2⅔ cups (400g) plain (all-purpose) flour,
    plus extra for dusting

300g cold unsalted butter, chopped

½ cup (120g) firmly packed brown sugar

½ teaspoon ground ginger

½ teaspoon ground cinnamon

2 eggs

2 teaspoons vanilla extract

To make the spiced brown sugar pastry, place the flour, butter, sugar, ginger and cinnamon in a food processor and process in short bursts until the mixture resembles coarse breadcrumbs. Add the eggs and vanilla and process until the pastry comes together. Turn out onto a generously floured bench and, using your hands, bring the dough together and divide it in half. Generously dust 4 sheets of non-stick baking paper with flour. Roll out each piece of dough between 2 sheets of the paper to 5mm thick. Refrigerate for 30 minutes.

Preheat oven to 160°C (325°F).

Place the apple, currants, sultanas, almonds, mixed peel, maple syrup, brown sugar, butter and schnapps in a medium saucepan over medium heat and cook, stirring occasionally, for 15 minutes or until the fruit is softened and the liquid is absorbed. Set aside to cool completely.

Lightly grease 24 x 2-tablespoon-capacity patty tins. Using a 7cm round cookie cutter lightly dusted in flour, cut 24 rounds from the dough (see *cook's tips*, page 210) and use them to line the tins. Re-roll the remaining dough between 2 generously floured sheets of non-stick baking paper to 5mm thick. Refrigerate for a further 15 minutes.

Divide the cooled fruit mixture between the pastry cases and brush the edges of the cases with egg. Using a 7cm fluted cookie cutter lightly dusted in flour, cut 24 rounds from the remaining dough. Using a 1cm round piping nozzle, cut a hole in the centre of each round.

Top the pies with the fluted rounds and press the edges to seal. Brush the tops with egg and sprinkle with the white sugar. Bake for 25–30 minutes or until golden.

Allow the pies to cool in the tins for 5 minutes, before turning out onto wire racks to cool completely. Dust with icing sugar to serve. MAKES 24

use floured cutters

line and fill the tins

cut pretty fluted tops

press the edges to seal

brush with a little egg

sprinkle with sugar

cook's tips

∘ While you could use a plain sweet shortcrust pastry for this recipe, the brown sugar and spices add a lovely warmth to the overall flavour of the pies.

∘ When making the pastry rounds, be sure to dust the cutters with flour. It makes cutting and lifting a breeze.

∘ If you don't have a fluted cutter, you can use a plain round cutter for the tops. The small hole in the centre is essential though, to let the steam escape while the pies are baking. It prevents the fruit mixture from spilling through the seams.

∘ We use both white, or granulated, sugar and icing, or confectioner's, sugar for dusting – the white sugar before baking adds a lovely crunch and the icing sugar adds extra sweetness.

∘ These fruit mince pies will keep in an airtight container at room temperature for 2–3 days.

dark chocolate truffles with caramel crunch

dark chocolate truffles with caramel crunch

⅔ cup (160ml) double (thick) cream
¾ cup (180g) firmly packed dark brown sugar
½ cup (110g) caster (superfine) sugar
50g unsalted butter
½ cup (175g) golden syrup
200g dark (70% cocoa) chocolate, melted
sea salt flakes, to serve
caramel crunch
⅓ cup (70g) coffee sugar crystals (see *note*, page 181)
1 tablespoon water

Preheat oven to 160°C (325°F).

To make the caramel crunch, place the coffee sugar crystals and the water in a bowl and mix well to combine. Spoon the sugar mixture onto a baking tray lined with non-stick baking paper. Bake for 30 minutes or until golden. Allow to cool on the tray, then break into small pieces and set aside.

Line a 10cm x 21cm loaf tin with non-stick baking paper. Place the cream, dark brown sugar, caster sugar, butter and golden syrup in a saucepan over medium heat and stir until smooth. Bring the mixture to a simmer and cook for around 15 minutes or until it reaches 124°C (255°F) on a sugar (candy) thermometer. Allow to cool for 5 minutes. Pour the mixture into the tin and refrigerate for 3–4 hours or until set. Slice into 20 bars.

Using two forks, dip each truffle bar into the melted chocolate, tapping off any excess, then place on a lightly oiled wire rack. Sprinkle with the caramel crunch and a pinch of sea salt flakes. Refrigerate until set, then serve. MAKES 20

Tip: Dark brown sugar gives these truffles their deep caramel flavour and chewy, moreish interior. They are well worth the effort.

rum and raisin truffles

½ cup (80g) raisins, chopped
⅓ cup (80ml) dark rum
¾ cup (180ml) pure cream
600g dark (70% cocoa) chocolate, finely chopped
1 cup (100g) cocoa

Combine the raisins and the rum in a small bowl. Set aside to soak.

Place the cream in a small saucepan over high heat and bring to the boil. Place the chocolate in a heatproof bowl and top with the hot cream. Place the bowl over a saucepan of simmering water (the bowl shouldn't touch the water) and, using a metal spoon, stir until melted and smooth. Add the raisin mixture and stir to combine. Allow to stand at room temperature for 10 minutes, before refrigerating for 2–3 hours or until just firm.

Roll 1-teaspoon portions of the mixture into balls[+] and place on a large baking tray. Dust with cocoa to serve.
MAKES 50

+ If the truffle mixture becomes too firm to roll, allow it to stand at room temperature for 15 minutes or until softened.

rum and raisin truffles

dark chocolate, clementine and honeycomb truffles

dark chocolate, clementine and honeycomb truffles

¾ cup (180ml) pure cream
800g dark (70% cocoa) chocolate, finely chopped
4 candied clementines (about 100g) (see *note*, page 195),
    finely chopped
2 teaspoons vegetable oil
1 cup (85g) store-bought honeycomb, crushed

Place the cream in a small saucepan over high heat and bring to the boil. Place 600g of the chocolate in a medium heatproof bowl and top with the hot cream. Place the bowl over a saucepan of simmering water (the bowl shouldn't touch the water) and, using a metal spoon, stir until melted and smooth.

Add the candied clementine and stir to combine. Allow to stand at room temperature for 10 minutes, then refrigerate for 2–3 hours or until just firm.

Roll 1-teaspoon portions of the mixture into balls and place on a large baking tray lined with non-stick baking paper. Refrigerate for 15 minutes or until set.

Place the remaining 200g of chocolate and the oil in a medium heatproof bowl over a saucepan of simmering water and, using a metal spoon, stir until melted and smooth.

Insert a toothpick into each truffle. Holding onto the toothpicks, dip the truffles into the melted chocolate, allowing any excess to drip off. Stick the truffles on their toothpicks into a piece of styrofoam or thick cardboard. Sprinkle with the honeycomb and refrigerate for 30 minutes or until set.

Remove the truffles from the toothpicks to serve.

MAKES 48

Tip: You can keep these truffles refrigerated for up to 2 weeks.

chocolate caramel truffles

1 cup (250ml) pure cream
½ cup (110g) caster (superfine) sugar
¼ cup (60ml) water
50g unsalted butter, softened
250g dark (70% cocoa) chocolate, roughly chopped
1 tablespoon butterscotch schnapps
200g dark (70% cocoa) chocolate, melted, extra

Place the cream in a small saucepan over medium heat and bring to a boil. Remove from the heat and set aside.

Place the sugar and water in a medium saucepan over low heat and stir until the sugar is dissolved. Increase the heat to medium and bring to the boil. Cook for 6 minutes or until a deep golden colour[+]. Remove from the heat and, working quickly, add the hot cream and the butter. Return the saucepan to the heat and stir to combine.

Place the chocolate in a bowl, pour in the caramel mixture and the schnapps and stir gently, until the chocolate is melted and the mixture is smooth. Place in a lightly greased 20cm square tin lined with non-stick baking paper and refrigerate for 2–3 hours or until set.

Roll 1-tablespoon portions of the mixture into balls and place on a baking tray lined with non-stick baking paper[++]. Freeze for 1 hour or until firm.

Dip the truffles in the extra melted chocolate and place on the tray. Refrigerate for 1 hour or until set.

MAKES APPROXIMATELY 22

+ It's important the caramel is deeply golden in colour, as adding the cream and butter will slow the cooking process. If the caramel is too pale, it will have a weak flavour. If it's too dark, it will taste bitter.

++ Dip a tablespoon in hot water and pat dry to help roll the mixture into balls. Use a skewer to help remove the truffles from the tablespoon.

Tip: You can keep these truffles refrigerated for up to 2 weeks.

chocolate caramel truffles

candy cane white chocolate bars

500g store-bought plain shortbread biscuits
180g unsalted butter, melted
360g white chocolate, melted
2 teaspoons vegetable oil
6 candy canes, coarsely crushed (see *note*, right)

Line a 20cm x 30cm slice tin with non-stick baking paper.
Place the biscuits in a food processor and process until fine.
Add the butter and process until combined. Transfer to the
tin and, using the back of a spoon, press the mixture evenly
into the base. Refrigerate for 15–20 minutes or until firm.
  Place the chocolate and oil in a small bowl and mix to
combine. Pour the chocolate over the biscuit base. Allow
to stand for 5 minutes or until just starting to set. Sprinkle
with the crushed candy cane and refrigerate for 1–2 hours or
until firm. Allow to stand at room temperature for 5 minutes
before cutting into bars with a hot knife to serve. SERVES 4–6

candy cane milkshakes

2 candy canes, finely crushed[+]
180g white chocolate, melted and cooled slightly
1 cup (250ml) cold milk
4 scoops (240ml) store-bought vanilla bean ice-cream
½ cup (125ml) pure cream, whipped to stiff peaks

Place the crushed candy canes on a small plate. Dip the
rim of 4 x ¾-cup-capacity (180ml) serving glasses into the
chocolate and press into the crushed candy cane. Place the
glasses upside-down on a tray until the chocolate has set.
  Place the milk, ice-cream and the remaining chocolate
in a blender and blend until smooth. Divide the milkshake
between the prepared glasses and top with the whipped
cream to serve. MAKES 4
+ *The best way to crush the candy canes is to place them in a
plastic sandwich bag and pound with a meat mallet or rolling pin
to the desired size. Humidity can affect the candy canes, making
them quite sticky once crushed. It helps to crush them just
before use.*

candy cane and brownie ice-cream

2 litres store-bought vanilla bean ice-cream
100g store-bought chocolate brownie (about 1 brownie),
   roughly chopped
8 candy canes, coarsely crushed (see *note*, page 218)

Place a 2-litre-capacity metal container in the freezer until
ready to use.

   Scoop the ice-cream into the bowl of an electric mixer
and beat on low speed for 1–2 minutes or until softened.
Add the brownie and three-quarters of the crushed candy
cane and fold to combine. Spoon into the chilled tin.
Sprinkle the ice-cream with the remaining crushed candy
cane and freeze for 3–4 hours or until set. MAKES 2 LITRES

cookies and cream candy cane truffles

10 candy canes
300g store-bought cream-filled chocolate biscuits
400g dark (70% cocoa) chocolate, melted
2 teaspoons vanilla extract
⅓ cup (80ml) pure cream

Place the candy canes in a food processor and process
until ground. Remove 2 tablespoons of the mixture and
set aside.

   Add the biscuits to the processor with the remaining
candy cane and process until finely ground. Add half the
chocolate and the vanilla and process until well combined.
Add the cream and process until just combined. Transfer the
mixture to a medium bowl and refrigerate for 15 minutes
or until firm.

   Line a baking tray with non-stick baking paper. Roll
1-tablespoon portions of the mixture into balls and dip into
the remaining chocolate, remelting if necessary. Place the
truffles on the tray and sprinkle with the reserved candy
cane. Refrigerate for 1 hour or until set, before serving.
MAKES 30

process to make a dough

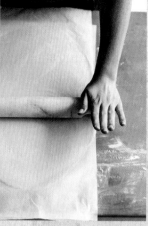

roll out half the dough

use star-shaped cutters

press the remaining dough

spread the base with jam

top with overlapping stars

raspberry and shortbread slice

250g cold unsalted butter, chopped
1 cup (160g) icing (confectioner's) sugar, sifted,
   plus extra for dusting
1½ cups (225g) plain (all-purpose) flour, sifted
½ cup (90g) white rice flour, sifted
   (see *cook's tips*, page 223)
1 teaspoon vanilla extract
1 x quantity cheat's raspberry jam, cooled
   (see *recipe*, page 223)+

Place the butter, sugar, both the flours and the vanilla
in a food processor and process until the dough just
comes together. Divide the dough in half, cover one half
and chill in the refrigerator. Roll the remaining half out
between 2 sheets of non-stick baking paper to 4mm thick.
Refrigerate for 30 minutes or until firm.
   Preheat oven to 160°C (325°F). Line a large baking tray
with non-stick baking paper.
   Using various-sized star-shaped cutters, cut shapes from
the rolled-out dough, reserving any scraps (see *cook's tips*,
page 223). Place the stars on the tray and refrigerate for
10–15 minutes or until firm enough to handle.
   Line a 20cm x 30cm slice tin with non-stick baking
paper, allowing 3cm of paper to extend above the edges.
Combine the dough scraps with the reserved chilled dough
and, using the back of a spoon, press it into the base of
the tin. Prick the base all over with a fork and bake for
20 minutes or until golden. Allow to cool for 15 minutes.
   Spread the jam over the shortbread base and top with
the stars, overlapping them slightly. Bake for 20 minutes or
until the stars are golden. Allow to cool completely in the tin.
   Remove the slice from the tin and dust with the extra
sugar to serve. SERVES 6–8
+ *You can use ¾ cup (240g) of store-bought raspberry jam*
in place of the cheat's jam on page 223, if you prefer.

raspberry and shortbread slice

cheat's raspberry jam

cheat's raspberry jam

2 cups (250g) frozen raspberries
¾ cup (165g) caster (superfine) sugar

Place the raspberries and sugar in a large non-stick frying pan over high heat. Cook, stirring, until the sugar is dissolved. Bring to the boil and cook, stirring continuously, for 8–10 minutes or until the jam has thickened slightly.

Allow the jam to cool completely before spreading onto the shortbread (see *recipe*, page 220), or spoon it into an airtight container immediately. MAKES 1 CUP

Tips: This cheat's jam will keep refrigerated, sealed in an airtight container, for up to 2–3 months. If you like, you can add some extra flavour to the jam – try finely grating in a little lemon rind, or scrape in the seeds of a vanilla bean.

cook's tips

∘ White rice flour is important in the shortbread recipe – it's what helps to give that classic crisp and crumbly texture to the biscuit when baked.

∘ When cutting the stars, dip the cookie cutters in a little flour to help prevent the dough from sticking.

∘ Pressing the dough into the tin with the back of a spoon will give it a smooth, even surface. Bake the base before spreading it with jam to help the shortbread stay crisp beneath the raspberry layer.

∘ This cheat's jam recipe, using frozen raspberries (no need to even thaw them!), is super simple to make and gives the shortbread slice a lovely tart flavour. With no extra additives – just fruit and sugar – you'll notice plenty of tiny seeds and a vibrant jewel-like colour.

∘ If you prefer, you can use ¾ cup (240g) of your favourite store-bought jam for the shortbread instead of the cheat's recipe – try cherry or strawberry.

∘ To save on stress during the Christmas season, why not make the shortbread dough in advance and freeze it? Cover it tightly and freeze for up to 2 months. Allow it to thaw in the fridge completely before baking.

chocolate and peppermint creams

chocolate and peppermint creams

150g unsalted butter, softened
½ cup (120g) firmly packed brown sugar
½ cup (175g) golden syrup
1½ cups (225g) plain (all-purpose) flour, sifted
¼ cup (25g) cocoa, sifted
1 teaspoon bicarbonate of (baking) soda, sifted
200g dark (70% cocoa) chocolate, chopped
peppermint cream
2½ cups (400g) icing (confectioner's) sugar, sifted
2 tablespoons milk
½ teaspoon peppermint extract

Place the butter, sugar and golden syrup in the bowl of an electric mixer and beat for 8–10 minutes or until pale and creamy. Add the flour, cocoa and bicarbonate of soda and beat until a smooth dough forms. Add the chocolate and mix well to combine. Refrigerate for 30 minutes or until firm.

Preheat oven to 180°C (350°F). Line 2 baking trays with non-stick baking paper.

Roll 1-tablespoon portions of the dough into balls. Place on the trays and flatten slightly, allowing room to spread. Bake for 10–12 minutes or until the cookies are just cracked on top. Allow to cool on the trays for 5 minutes. Transfer to wire racks to cool completely.

To make the peppermint cream, place the sugar, milk and peppermint extract in the clean bowl of an electric mixer and beat for 3–4 minutes or until smooth.

Spread the underside of half the biscuits with the peppermint cream and sandwich with the remaining biscuits to serve. MAKES 18

Tip: Filled peppermint creams will keep in an airtight container for up to 1 week. It helps to place non-stick baking paper between the cookies to ensure they don't stick together.

sour cherry and lemon shortbread fingers

120g unsalted butter, softened
1 cup (220g) caster (superfine) sugar
1 egg
1 teaspoon vanilla extract
1¾ cups (260g) plain (all-purpose) flour
1 teaspoon baking powder
1 tablespoon finely grated lemon rind
sour cherry jam
½ cup (100g) dried sour cherries
¼ cup (80g) store-bought strawberry jam
1 tablespoon caster (superfine) sugar

To make the sour cherry jam, place the cherries, jam and sugar in a food processor and process until a rough paste forms. Transfer to a small saucepan over high heat, bring to the boil and cook, stirring, for 2 minutes or until thickened. Remove from the heat and set aside to cool completely.

Place the butter and sugar in the bowl of an electric mixer and beat for 4 minutes or until pale and fluffy. Add the egg and vanilla and beat to combine. Add the flour, baking powder and lemon rind and mix until just combined.

Divide the dough in half and roll each piece out between 2 sheets of non-stick baking paper to make 2 x 16cm x 22cm rectangles. Use a ruler to help you check the rectangles are the correct size and place them on the trays. Freeze for 30 minutes or until firm.

Spread the sour cherry jam over 1 rectangle of dough and top with the remaining rectangle. Wrap and freeze for a further 1 hour or until very firm.

Preheat oven to 180°C (350°F). Line 2 large baking trays with non-stick baking paper.

Remove the wrap and, using a sharp knife, trim and discard the edges from the dough. Using the ruler as a guide, cut the dough into 1cm-thick lengths and place on the trays. Bake for 10–12 minutes or until golden. Allow the shortbread to cool on the trays before serving. MAKES 20

Tip: You can freeze these cookies in an airtight container for up to 3 months. Defrost at room temperature for 20–30 minutes or heat them in a 160°C (325°F) oven for 10 minutes or until warmed through.

sour cherry and lemon shortbread fingers

spiced brown sugar cookies

spiced brown sugar cookies

2 cups (320g) icing (confectioner's) sugar
3 teaspoons ground cinnamon
2¼ cups (335g) plain (all-purpose) flour
½ teaspoon ground ginger
½ teaspoon ground allspice
¼ teaspoon ground cloves
¼ teaspoon ground nutmeg
¼ teaspoon bicarbonate of (baking) soda
120g unsalted butter, softened
1 cup (240g) firmly packed brown sugar
⅓ cup (115g) golden syrup
1 egg
1 teaspoon vanilla extract

Preheat oven to 180°C (350°F). Line 2 large baking trays with non-stick baking paper.

Place the icing sugar and 2 teaspoons of the cinnamon in a large bowl. Mix to combine and set aside.

Place the flour and the remaining 1 teaspoon of cinnamon in a medium bowl. Add the ginger, allspice, cloves, nutmeg and bicarbonate of soda. Mix to combine and set aside.

Place the butter, brown sugar and golden syrup in the bowl of an electric mixer and beat for 3 minutes or until pale and fluffy. Add the egg and vanilla and beat to combine. Add the flour mixture and beat until just combined. Roll 1-tablespoon portions of the dough into balls and place on the trays, allowing room to spread. Bake for 8–10 minutes or until golden and slightly cracked. Transfer to wire racks to cool for 10 minutes. Place the biscuits in the spiced sugar and gently toss to coat. Return to the racks and allow to cool completely before serving. MAKES 36

Tip: These cookies will keep in an airtight container for up to 1 week. It helps to place non-stick baking paper between the cookies to ensure they don't stick together.

coconut and jam hearts

125g unsalted butter, chopped
½ cup (110g) caster (superfine) sugar
1 egg
1 teaspoon vanilla extract
1½ cups (225g) plain (all-purpose) flour, sifted
½ teaspoon baking powder, sifted
½ cup (40g) desiccated coconut
icing (confectioner's) sugar, for dusting
½ cup (160g) store-bought raspberry or strawberry jam

Place the butter and sugar in the bowl of an electric mixer and beat for 6 minutes or until pale and creamy. Add the egg and vanilla and beat until well combined. Add the flour, baking powder and coconut and beat for a further 1 minute or until well combined. Refrigerate for 30 minutes or until firm.

Preheat oven to 180°C (350°F). Line 2 large baking trays with non-stick baking paper.

Divide the dough in half and roll each portion out between 2 sheets of non-stick baking paper to 3mm thick. Using a 7cm round cookie cutter, cut 24 rounds from the dough. Place on the trays. Using a 4cm heart-shaped cutter, cut and discard heart shapes from the centre of 12 of the rounds[+]. Bake for 8–10 minutes or until golden. Allow to cool on the trays.

Dust the cut-out rounds with icing sugar. Spread the plain rounds with jam and sandwich with the cut-out rounds.
MAKES 12

+ You can bake the little cut-out hearts, if you wish – they'll need a bit less time in the oven. They're ready when they're golden.

Tip: Store these cookies in an airtight container for up to 1 week. It helps to place non-stick baking paper between the cookies to ensure they don't stick together.

coconut and jam hearts

Give the gift of a *home-baked treat* this festive season,
like these addictive crackle cookies. Made with *a dusting of
sugary snow* and nestled in these *enchanting little houses,* you'll
enjoy making these cookies almost as much as eating them.

brown butter crackle cookies

150g unsalted butter, chopped
1¼ cups (200g) rapadura sugar
2 eggs
2 teaspoons vanilla extract
2½ cups (375g) plain (all-purpose) flour
1 teaspoon baking powder
1 teaspoon ground cinnamon
pure icing (confectioner's) sugar, for rolling

Place the butter in a small saucepan over medium heat and cook until foaming. Whisk for 2–3 minutes or until a deep golden colour. Set aside to cool slightly.

Place the butter and the rapadura sugar in the bowl of an electric mixer and beat until combined. Add the eggs and vanilla and beat well. Sift in the flour, baking powder and cinnamon and beat on low speed until combined. Cover the cookie dough loosely with a tea towel and refrigerate for 1 hour or until firm.

Preheat oven to 180°C (350°F). Line 2 baking trays with non-stick baking paper.

Sift the icing sugar into a shallow bowl. Roll 1-tablespoon portions of the cookie dough into balls, then roll in the icing sugar to coat them.

Place the dough balls on the prepared trays and bake for 10–12 minutes or until the cookies are just golden and set. Allow to cool on the trays before serving. MAKES 26
Tip: Get crafty and make these sweet gift boxes for your crackle cookies. Download, print and use scissors to cut out the template at donnahay.com.au/files/DH01_Festive_house_gift-box_template..pdf

brown butter crackle cookies

caramel shortbread sandwiches

150g unsalted butter, softened
⅓ cup (55g) icing (confectioner's) sugar, sifted
1 teaspoon vanilla extract
1½ cups (225g) plain (all-purpose) flour, sifted
2 tablespoons cornflour (cornstarch), sifted
⅔ cup (200g) store-bought good-quality dulce de leche
    (see note, page 129)

Place the butter, sugar and vanilla in the bowl of an electric mixer and beat for 8–10 minutes or until pale and creamy. Add the flour and cornflour and beat until a smooth dough forms. Roll the dough out between 2 sheets of non-stick baking paper to 5mm thick and refrigerate for 30 minutes or until firm.

Preheat oven to 180°C (350°F). Line 2 large baking trays with non-stick baking paper.

Using a 4.5cm round cookie cutter, cut 40 rounds from the dough. Place the cookies on the trays. Bake for 10–12 minutes or until just golden. Allow to cool completely on the trays.

Spread half the shortbreads with the dulce de leche and sandwich with the remaining shortbreads. MAKES 20

cranberry shortbread hearts

150g unsalted butter, chopped and softened
⅓ cup (55g) icing (confectioner's) sugar, sifted
1 teaspoon vanilla extract
1½ cups (225g) plain (all-purpose) flour, sifted
2 tablespoons cornflour (cornstarch), sifted
¾ cup (100g) dried cranberries, chopped

Place the butter, sugar and vanilla in the bowl of an electric mixer and beat for 8 minutes or until pale and creamy. Add the flour, cornflour and cranberries and beat until just combined. Roll the mixture out between 2 sheets of non-stick baking paper to 3mm thick. Refrigerate for 30 minutes or until firm.

Preheat oven to 160°C (325°F). Line 2 large baking trays with non-stick baking paper.

Using an 8cm heart-shaped cutter, cut 14 hearts from the dough, re-rolling as necessary. Place the hearts on the trays. Using a 3mm round piping nozzle, cut a hole in the top of each cookie. Bake for 12–14 minutes or until golden. Allow to cool on the trays.

Thread the hearts with ribbon to hang or serve. MAKES 14

cranberry and pistachio biscotti

2 cups (300g) plain (all-purpose) flour, sifted
1½ teaspoons baking powder, sifted
¾ cup (165g) caster (superfine) sugar
3 eggs, lightly whisked
2 teaspoons vanilla extract
1 tablespoon finely grated orange rind
1 cup (140g) dried cranberries
1 cup (140g) shelled unsalted pistachios

Preheat oven to 160°C (325°F). Line 2 large baking trays
with non-stick baking paper.

Place the flour, baking powder and sugar in a large bowl
and mix to combine. Add the eggs, vanilla, orange rind,
cranberries and pistachios and mix until a smooth
dough forms.

Turn the dough out onto on a well-floured surface and
knead until smooth. Divide in half and roll each piece into
a 20cm log. Flatten slightly and place on the trays. Bake
for 30–35 minutes or until firm. Allow to cool. Use a large
serrated knife to slice the logs into 3mm-thick biscotti.
Place the biscotti on the trays and bake for a further
8–10 minutes or until golden and crisp. Allow to cool on
the trays. MAKES 80

lemon and almond cookies

90g unsalted butter, softened
1 cup (220g) raw or Demerara sugar
1 cup (120g) almond meal (ground almonds)
1 cup (150g) plain (all-purpose) flour
½ teaspoon baking powder
¼ cup (60ml) lemon juice
2 tablespoons finely grated lemon rind
1 teaspoon vanilla extract
icing (confectioner's) sugar, for dusting

Place the butter and sugar in the bowl of an electric mixer
and beat for 5 minutes or until pale. Add the almond meal,
flour, baking powder, lemon juice, rind and vanilla. Beat for
2 minutes or until a dough forms. Roll out between 2 sheets
of non-stick baking paper to 5mm thick and refrigerate for
30 minutes.

Preheat oven to 160°C (325°F). Line 2 baking trays with
non-stick baking paper.

Using an 8.5cm round fluted cutter, cut 12 rounds from
the dough. Using a 3.5cm round cutter, cut and discard the
centre from each cookie. Place on the trays and bake for
10–12 minutes or until golden. Allow to cool on the trays.
Dust with icing sugar to serve. MAKES 12

gingerbread village

basic gingerbread cookie dough

125g unsalted butter, softened
½ cup (120g) firmly packed brown sugar
⅔ cup (230g) golden syrup+
2½ cups (375g) plain (all-purpose) flour, sifted
1 teaspoon bicarbonate of (baking) soda, sifted
2 teaspoons ground ginger
1 teaspoon mixed spice

Place the butter and sugar in the bowl of an electric mixer and beat for 10–12 minutes or until pale and creamy. Scrape down the sides of the bowl, then add the golden syrup, flour, bicarbonate of soda, ginger and mixed spice. Beat until a smooth dough forms. MAKES 1 QUANTITY
+ *If you can't find golden syrup, use 1⅓ cups (330 ml) pure maple syrup in its place.*
Tips: See the recipes that follow for how to roll out, cut and bake various gingerbread treats. If the dough feels too soft at any stage, you can refrigerate it for a few minutes before continuing. Freeze any wrapped leftover dough for up to 2 months.

chocolate gingerbread cookie dough

125g unsalted butter, chopped and softened
½ cup (120g) firmly packed brown sugar
⅔ cup (230g) golden syrup (see *note*, above)
2⅓ cups (350g) plain (all-purpose) flour, sifted
⅓ cup (35g) cocoa, sifted
1 teaspoon bicarbonate of (baking) soda, sifted
2 teaspoons ground ginger
1 teaspoon mixed spice

Place the butter and sugar in the bowl of an electric mixer and beat for 10–12 minutes or until pale and creamy. Scrape down the sides of the bowl and add the golden syrup, flour, cocoa, bicarbonate of soda, ginger and mixed spice. Beat until a smooth dough forms (see *tips*, above).
MAKES 1 QUANTITY

gingerbread village

250g unsalted butter, softened
1 cup (240g) firmly packed brown sugar
1⅓ cups (460g) golden syrup (see *note*, left)
5 cups (750g) plain (all-purpose) flour, sifted
2 teaspoons bicarbonate of (baking) soda, sifted
1 tablespoon ground ginger
2 teaspoons ground cinnamon

Place the butter and sugar in the bowl of an electric mixer and beat for 10–12 minutes or until pale and creamy. Scrape down the sides of the bowl. Add the golden syrup, flour, bicarbonate of soda, ginger and cinnamon. Beat until a smooth dough forms.

Roll out the dough between 2 sheets of non-stick baking paper to 4mm thick. Refrigerate for 30 minutes or until firm.

Preheat oven to 140°C (275°F). Line 3 baking trays with non-stick baking paper. For the gingerbread houses, download, print and use scissors to cut out the templates at *donnahay.com.au/files/DH01_Festive_gingerbread_village_templates.pdf*. For the people, tree and animals, use a variety of cookie cutters+. You can use the picture as a guide to make your own gingerbread family++.

Place the gingerbread houses on the trays and bake for 35–50 minutes (depending on their size) or until golden. Bake the gingerbread shapes for 15–20 minutes or until golden. Allow to cool on the trays. MAKES 20
+ *Cookie cutters in various shapes and sizes are available to buy from homewares retailers, cake decorating stores or online.*
++ *If the dough feels too soft at any stage, you can refrigerate it for a few minutes. Wrap and freeze any leftover dough for up to 2 months.*

gingerbread snowmen

1 x quantity basic gingerbread dough (see *recipe*, page 235)

Roll the dough out between 2 sheets of non-stick baking paper to 4mm thick. Refrigerate for 30 minutes or until firm.

Preheat oven to 160°C (325°F). Line a baking tray with non-stick baking paper.

Using 10cm and 9cm snowman-shaped cutters, cut 20 shapes from the dough. Place on the tray and bake for 10–12 minutes or until golden. Allow to cool on the tray, before serving. MAKES 20

gingerbread antlers

1 x quantity basic gingerbread dough (see *recipe*, page 235)

Roll the dough out between 2 sheets of non-stick baking paper to 4mm thick. Refrigerate for 30 minutes or until firm.

Preheat oven to 160°C (325°F). Line a baking tray with non-stick baking paper.

Using an 11cm antler-shaped cutter, cut 14 shapes from the dough. Place on the tray and bake for 10–12 minutes or until golden. Allow to cool on the tray, before serving. MAKES 14

mixed gingerbread christmas trees

1 x quantity basic gingerbread dough (see *recipe*, page 235)
1 x quantity chocolate gingerbread dough
  (see *recipe*, page 235)
chocolate icing
2 cups (320g) icing (confectioner's) sugar, sifted
¼ cup (25g) cocoa, sifted
2 tablespoons boiling water, plus 1 tablespoon extra

Roll each dough out between 2 sheets of non-stick baking paper to 5mm thick. Refrigerate for 30 minutes or until firm.

Preheat oven to 140°C (275°F). Line 2 large baking trays with non-stick baking paper. Download, print and use scissors to cut out the templates at *donnahay.com.au/files/ Gingerbread_Christmas_Trees.pdf*. Alternatively, create your own templates using the measurements below[+].

Using the templates as a guide and a small sharp knife, cut the panels for 1 small, 1 medium and 1 large tree from each sheet of dough, re-rolling as necessary. Using a 2cm and 3cm star-shaped cutter, cut 6 stars from the dough of your choice.

Place the trees and stars on the trays and bake for 23–25 minutes or until golden and dry to the touch. Allow to cool completely on the trays.

To make the chocolate icing, place the sugar and cocoa in a medium bowl. Gradually add the water and whisk until the mixture is smooth and pliable, only adding the extra water if necessary.

Spoon the icing into a piping bag fitted with a 5mm round nozzle. Trim to straighten the edges of the trees, using a small serrated knife, and pipe icing onto each long edge. Assemble 3 matching sides together, pressing gently to attach, and allow to stand for 30 minutes or until set.

Pipe a little icing onto the top of each tree and attach the stars to serve. MAKES 6

+ *Print the templates from donnahay.com, or use a ruler and pencil to create your own. Draw 1 panel of each-sized tree on paper. A small tree is 17cm tall and has an 8cm-wide base. A medium tree is 22cm tall and has a 9cm-wide base. A large tree is 29cm tall and has a 10cm-wide base. Use scissors to cut out the 3 templates. Use the templates to cut 3 panels for each tree from each sheet of dough.*

mixed gingerbread christmas trees

gingerbread men ice-cream sandwiches

gingerbread men ice-cream sandwiches

4 litres store-bought vanilla bean ice-cream
125g unsalted butter, chopped and softened
½ cup (120g) firmly packed brown sugar
⅔ cup (230g) golden syrup
2½ cups (375g) plain (all-purpose) flour, sifted
2 teaspoons ground ginger
1 teaspoon bicarbonate of (baking) soda

Scoop the ice-cream into the bowl of an electric mixer and beat on low speed until softened. Spoon into a 25cm x 35cm baking dish and smooth the top. Cover with non-stick baking paper and freeze for 3–4 hours or until set.

Place the butter and sugar in the clean bowl of an electric mixer and beat for 8–10 minutes or until pale and creamy. Add the golden syrup, flour, ginger and bicarbonate of soda and beat until the mixture just comes together to form a smooth dough. Roll the dough out between 2 sheets of non-stick baking paper to 4mm thick and refrigerate for 30 minutes.

Preheat oven to 190°C (375°F). Line 2 baking trays with non-stick baking paper.

Using a 12cm gingerbread man-shaped cutter, cut 16 shapes from the dough. Place on the trays and bake for 8–10 minutes or until golden. Allow to cool on the trays.

Lightly grease the cutter and cut 8 men from the ice-cream. Working quickly, sandwich the ice-cream between the cooled cookies and freeze until ready to serve. **MAKES 8**
Tip: You will have gingerbread cookie dough left over. Either wrap and freeze for up to 2 months for later use, or roll it out and cut into shapes to bake with the gingerbread men.

basic vanilla snap cookie dough

125g unsalted butter, softened
½ cup (110g) caster (superfine) sugar
1 egg
2 teaspoons vanilla extract
2 cups (300g) plain (all-purpose) flour, sifted

Place the butter and sugar in the bowl of an electric mixer and beat for 6–8 minutes or until pale and creamy. Add the egg and vanilla and beat for a further 2–3 minutes or until well combined. Add the flour and beat until the mixture just comes together to form a smooth dough. Cover and refrigerate for 30 minutes or until firm.
MAKES 1 QUANTITY
Tip: See the recipes that follow for how to roll out, cut and bake various vanilla snap cookies.

Give your *favourite festive biscuits* a fresh makeover by sandwiching them with ice-cream and watch as they *effortlessly transform* from afternoon tea treat to *delicious dessert.*

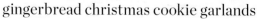

gingerbread christmas cookie garlands

1 x quantity basic gingerbread dough (see *recipe*, page 235)
1 x quantity chocolate gingerbread dough
  (see *recipe*, page 235)

Roll each dough out between 2 sheets of non-stick
baking paper to 5mm thick. Refrigerate for 30 minutes
or until firm.

Preheat oven to 140°C (275°F). Line 2 large baking trays
with non-stick baking paper.

Using various-shaped 5cm cutters, cut a selection of
gingerbread men, Christmas trees, stars and snowmen,
re-rolling the dough as necessary. Use a 6mm round
piping nozzle to cut 2 holes in the centre of each shape.
Place on the trays and bake for 20–22 minutes or until
golden and dry to the touch. Allow to cool completely
on the trays.

Thread half the cookies onto a length of ribbon and tie the
ends to secure. Repeat with the remaining cookies+. MAKES 2
+ *This recipe is designed to make 2 x 32-cookie garlands.*
Tips: You can store the gingerbread cookies in an airtight
container for up to 1–2 weeks. Hang them on Christmas Eve.
Cookie cutters in various shapes and sizes are available to buy
from homewares retailers, cake-decorating stores and online.

gingerbread men wreaths

1 x quantity basic gingerbread dough (see *recipe*, page 235)

Roll the dough out between 2 sheets of non-stick
baking paper to 5mm thick. Refrigerate for 30 minutes
or until firm.

Preheat oven to 140°C (275°F). Line 2 large baking
trays with non-stick baking paper.

Using a 7cm gingerbread man-shaped cutter, cut
22 shapes from the dough, re-rolling as necessary. Arrange
on the trays to form 2 rings, with alternate hands and feet
overlapping. Bake for 30 minutes or until golden and dry
to the touch. Allow to cool completely on the trays.

Thread lengths of ribbon through the gingerbread men,
leaving enough excess to hang the wreaths. MAKES 2
Tip: You can store the gingerbread wreaths in an airtight
container for up to 1–2 weeks. Hang them on Christmas Eve.

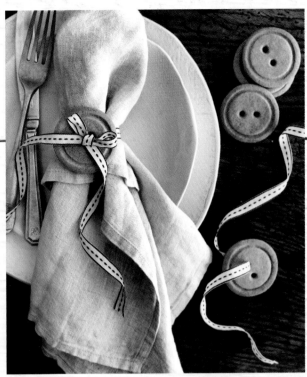

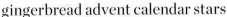

gingerbread advent calendar stars

1 x quantity basic gingerbread dough (see *recipe*, page 235)
1½ cups (240g) icing (confectioner's) sugar, sifted
1 eggwhite

Roll the dough out between 2 sheets of non-stick baking paper to 5mm thick. Refrigerate for 30 minutes or until firm.

Preheat oven to 140°C (275°F). Line 2 large baking trays with non-stick baking paper.

Using star-shaped cutters, cut 8 x 5.5cm stars, 8 x 6.5cm stars, 4 x 7.5cm stars and 5 x 9.5cm stars from the dough[+]. Use the tip of a 6mm round piping nozzle to cut a hole in the top of each star. Place the stars on the trays and bake for 18–20 minutes or until golden and dry to the touch. Allow to cool completely on the trays.

Place the sugar and eggwhite in a medium bowl and mix to combine. Spoon into a piping bag fitted with a 2mm round nozzle. Pipe borders on the stars. Number them from 1 to 25. Allow to set and thread onto ribbon or string to hang. MAKES 25

+ *There's enough gingerbread dough to make 40 cookies. Freeze the leftover dough or cut and bake extra gingerbread cookies.*

gingerbread buttons

1 x quantity basic gingerbread dough (see *recipe*, page 235)

Roll the dough out between 2 sheets of non-stick baking paper to 5mm thick. Refrigerate for 30 minutes or until firm.

Preheat oven to 140°C (275°F). Line 2 large baking trays with non-stick baking paper.

Using a 5cm cookie cutter, cut 32 rounds from the dough, re-rolling as necessary. Using a 3cm round cutter, indent to mark a border on each round. Using the tip of a 6mm round piping nozzle, cut 2 holes from the centre of each cookie. Place on the trays and bake for 18–20 minutes or until golden and dry to the touch. Allow to cool completely on the trays. Thread the cookies onto ribbon and use as decorations or napkin rings. MAKES 32

Tips: Extra cookies will keep in an airtight container for up to 1–2 weeks. You could also use the chocolate gingerbread cookie dough (see recipe, page 235) to make these buttons, if you prefer.

gingerbread heart garlands

1 x quantity basic gingerbread dough (see *recipe*, page 235)

Roll the dough out between 2 sheets of non-stick baking paper to 5mm thick. Refrigerate for 30 minutes or until firm.

Preheat oven to 160°C (325°F). Line 2 large baking trays with non-stick baking paper.

Using a 3.5cm heart-shaped cutter, cut 80 hearts from the dough, re-rolling as necessary. Using the tip of a 3mm round piping nozzle, cut a hole in the top of each heart. Place on the trays and bake for 12–15 minutes or until golden and dry to the touch. Allow to cool completely on the trays. Thread onto string or ribbon to hang[+]. **MAKES 8**
+ *This recipe is designed to make 8 x 10-cookie garlands, but you can choose to hang them whichever way you like.*

lemon and vanilla snowflakes

1 x quantity basic vanilla snap dough (see *recipe*, page 239)
1 tablespoon finely grated lemon rind
1 cup (160g) icing (confectioner's) sugar, sifted
1 tablespoon boiling water

Follow the basic vanilla snap dough recipe, adding the lemon rind with the egg.

Roll the dough out between 2 sheets of non-stick baking paper to 3mm thick. Refrigerate for 30 minutes or until firm.

Preheat oven to 140°C (275°F). Line 2 large baking trays with non-stick baking paper.

Using assorted snowflake-shaped cutters, cut 25 shapes from the dough, re-rolling as necessary. Using the tip of a 2mm round piping nozzle, cut a hole in the top of each snowflake. Place on the trays and bake for 8–10 minutes or until golden. Allow to cool completely on the trays.

Place the sugar and water in a small bowl and mix until smooth. Spoon into a piping bag fitted with a 2mm round nozzle and pipe onto snowflakes to decorate. Allow to set before threading with string or ribbon to hang. **MAKES 25**

chocolate-chip gingerbread cookies

100g dark (70% cocoa) chocolate, chopped
1 x quantity basic gingerbread dough (see *recipe*, page 235)

Preheat oven to 160°C (325°F). Line 2 large baking trays with non-stick baking paper.

Add the chocolate to the basic gingerbread dough and gently mix to combine. Roll 1-tablespoon portions of the mixture into balls and place on the trays, allowing room to spread. Flatten slightly and bake for 10–12 minutes or until golden. Allow to cool completely on the trays, before serving. **MAKES 24**

Tip: Paired with a glass of milk, these cookies make the perfect treat to leave out for Santa on Christmas Eve. You can bake them ahead of time and store in an airtight container for 1–2 weeks.

vanilla star wreaths

1 x quantity basic vanilla snap dough (see *recipe*, page 239)
icing (confectioner's) sugar, for dusting

Roll the dough out between 2 sheets of non-stick baking paper to 3mm thick. Refrigerate for 30 minutes or until firm.

Preheat oven to 140°C (275°F). Line 2 large baking trays with non-stick baking paper.

Trace 2 x 14cm circles onto each sheet and turn the paper over to prevent any pencil marks transferring.

Using an 8cm star-shaped cutter, cut 28 stars from the dough, re-rolling as necessary. Arrange 7 stars around each circle, overlapping the tips to create wreath shapes. Bake for 20–25 minutes or until golden. Allow to cool completely on the trays.

Dust with icing sugar and tie the wreaths with string or ribbon to hang. **MAKES 4**

Tip: Store wreaths in an airtight container for up to 2–3 days and hang them on Christmas Eve.

gingerbread reindeer

1 x quantity basic gingerbread dough (see *recipe*, page 235)

Roll the dough out between 2 sheets of non-stick baking paper to 4mm thick. Refrigerate for 30 minutes or until firm.

Preheat oven to 160°C (325°F). Line a baking tray with non-stick baking paper.

Using 7cm and 5cm deer-shaped cutters, cut 32 shapes from the dough. Place on the tray and bake for 8–10 minutes or until golden. Allow to cool on the trays, before serving. **MAKES 32**

spiced vanilla reindeer

1 x quantity basic vanilla snap dough (see *recipe*, page 239)
1 teaspoon ground cinnamon
1 teaspoon mixed spice
icing
½ cup (80g) icing (confectioner's) sugar, sifted
2 teaspoons boiling water

Follow the basic vanilla dough recipe, adding the cinnamon and mixed spice with the flour. Roll the dough out between 2 sheets of non-stick baking paper to 5mm thick and refrigerate for 30 minutes or until firm.

Preheat oven to 160°C (325°F). Line 2 large baking trays with non-stick baking paper.

Using a 7cm deer-shaped cutter, cut 32 shapes from the dough, re-rolling as necessary. Place on the trays and bake for 8–10 minutes or until golden. Allow to cool completely on the trays.

To make the icing, place the sugar and water in a small bowl and mix until smooth.

Spoon into a piping bag fitted with a 2mm round nozzle and pipe a nose and three tail spots on each deer to decorate. Allow to set before serving. **MAKES 32**

chocolate cookie christmas tree

1 x quantity basic vanilla snap dough (see *recipe*, page 239)
¼ cup (25g) cocoa, sifted
icing (confectioner's) sugar, for dusting
icing
½ cup (80g) icing (confectioner's) sugar, sifted
2 teaspoons boiling water

Follow the basic vanilla dough recipe, adding the cocoa with the flour. Roll the dough out between 2 sheets of non-stick baking paper to 3mm thick. Refrigerate for 30 minutes or until firm.

Preheat oven to 160°C (325°F). Line 2 large baking trays with non-stick baking paper.

Use 12cm, 11cm, 10cm, 9cm, 8cm, 7cm, 6cm, 5cm, 4cm and 3cm six-pointed star-shaped cutters to cut 3 stars of each size from the dough, re-rolling as necessary. Place on the trays and bake for 10 minutes or until dry to the touch. Allow to cool on the trays for 5 minutes. Transfer to wire racks to cool completely.

To make the icing, place the sugar and water in a small bowl and mix until smooth.

Stack the stars from largest to smallest on a serving plate, securing each star with a little of the icing. Dust the tree with icing sugar to serve. **MAKES 1**

Tip: Cookie cutters in various shapes and sizes are available to buy from homewares retailers, cake-decorating stores and online.

spiced vanilla reindeer + chocolate cookie christmas tree

dill, rosemary and yoghurt biscuits

dill, rosemary and yoghurt biscuits

1¾ cups (210g) wholemeal (whole-wheat) spelt flour
½ cup (140g) plain thick yoghurt
1 cup (125g) finely grated firm goat's cheese
1 teaspoon sea salt flakes
½ teaspoon cracked black pepper
50g unsalted butter, softened
¼ cup dill leaves, finely chopped
¼ cup rosemary leaves, finely chopped

Place the flour, yoghurt, cheese, salt, pepper and butter in a food processor and process until the mixture comes together. Add the dill and rosemary and pulse until just combined.

Turn the dough out and bring together to form a ball. Roll out between 2 sheets of non-stick baking paper to 4mm thick. Refrigerate for 30 minutes.

Preheat oven to 180°C (350°F). Line 2 large baking trays with non-stick baking paper.

Using a 7cm round cookie cutter, cut 28 rounds from the dough, re-rolling as necessary. Place on the trays. Bake for 15 minutes or until firm and golden. Allow to cool on the trays or transfer to wire racks before serving. MAKES 28

basil lavosh

1 teaspoon dry yeast
½ cup (125ml) lukewarm water
1 teaspoon caster (superfine) sugar
2 cups (300g) 00 flour, plus extra for dusting
1 teaspoon sea salt flakes, plus extra for sprinkling
¼ cup (60ml) extra virgin olive oil, plus extra for brushing
1 eggwhite, lightly whisked
2 cups basil leaves

Place the yeast, water and sugar in a small bowl and mix to combine. Set aside in a warm place for 5–10 minutes or until the surface is foamy.

Place the flour and salt in a large bowl and mix to combine. Make a well in the centre and add the oil and the yeast mixture. Mix until a dough forms. Turn the dough out and knead for 5–6 minutes or until smooth and elastic. Place in a large lightly oiled bowl, cover and set aside in a warm place for 20 minutes or until risen slightly.

Preheat oven to 180°C (350°F). Line 2 large baking trays with non-stick baking paper.

Divide the dough into 8 pieces and roll each piece out on a lightly floured surface to make a 1mm-thick oval shape. Lightly brush each lavosh with eggwhite and top with the basil leaves, pressing to secure. Place 2 lavosh on each tray, brush with the extra oil and sprinkle with the extra salt. Bake for 12 minutes or until puffed and golden brown. Transfer to wire racks and repeat with the remaining lavosh, extra oil and salt. Allow to cool before serving. MAKES 8

basil lavosh

burnt butter, honey and sage crackers

burnt butter, honey and sage crackers

1¼ cups (185g) wholemeal (whole-wheat) plain
  (all-purpose) flour
1½ cups (135g) rolled oats
½ cup (40g) finely grated parmesan
1 teaspoon sea salt flakes
1 egg
200g unsalted butter, chopped
¼ cup (90g) honey
1 bunch sage (about 6 sprigs), leaves picked
1 eggwhite, extra

Place the flour, oats, parmesan, salt and egg in a food
processor and process until the oats are finely chopped.
   Place the butter, honey and half the sage in a small
non-stick frying pan over high heat. Cook for 2–3 minutes
or until the butter starts to foam. Remove from the heat
and allow to cool slightly. Remove and discard the sage
and add the butter mixture to the food processor. Process
until the mixture just comes together. Turn the dough
out and bring together to form a ball. Roll out between
2 sheets of non-stick baking paper to make a 4mm-thick
30cm x 40cm rectangle.
   Pick the remaining sage leaves from the stalks. Remove
the top sheet of paper from the dough. Lightly brush the
dough with the eggwhite and top with the sage leaves,
pressing gently to secure. Return the paper to the dough
and gently roll over it to secure the leaves. Remove and
discard the top sheet of paper, cut the dough into squares
and prick each with a fork. Using the paper to help you,
slide the dough onto a large baking tray and refrigerate
for 30 minutes.
   Preheat oven to 160°C (325°F).
   Bake the crackers for 20 minutes or until golden and
crisp. Allow to cool on the tray before breaking into
squares to serve. MAKES 30

mixed olive and thyme biscotti

3 cups (450g) plain (all-purpose) flour
2 teaspoons baking powder
1½ cups (200g) pitted mixed olives+, sliced
½ teaspoon sea salt flakes
2 tablespoons thyme leaves, finely chopped
1 cup (80g) finely grated pecorino
2 eggs
½ cup (125ml) milk

Preheat oven to 160°C (325°F). Line a 20cm square slice
tin with non-stick baking paper.
   Place the flour, baking powder, olives, salt, thyme and
pecorino in a large bowl and mix to combine. Make a well
in the centre, add the eggs and milk and mix well to
combine. Press the mixture into the base of the tin. Bake
for 30 minutes or until golden. Remove from the tin and
set aside to cool slightly.
   Line 3 large baking trays with non-stick baking paper.
Using a serrated knife, slice the dough into 2mm-thick
pieces and place on the trays. Bake for 20 minutes or until
crisp and golden. Transfer to wire racks to cool completely,
before serving. MAKES 40
+ Try a mix of kalamata and Sicilian olives, or use your
favourite combination.

mixed olive and thyme biscotti

currant, juniper and blue cheese biscuits + parmesan, fennel and lemon thyme biscuits
basic parmesan biscuits + three-cheese biscuits + parmesan and pink peppercorn biscuits

basic parmesan biscuits

1 cup (150g) plain (all-purpose) flour
1 cup (80g) finely grated parmesan
½ cup (45g) rolled oats
100g cold unsalted butter, chopped
½ teaspoon sea salt flakes
1 egg yolk
1½ tablespoons iced water

Place the flour, parmesan, oats, butter and salt in a food processor and pulse until the mixture resembles fine breadcrumbs. Add the egg yolk and water and process until the mixture comes together. Turn the dough out and bring together to form a ball. Roll out between 2 sheets of non-stick baking paper to 5mm thick. Refrigerate for 30 minutes.

Preheat oven to 180°C (350°F). Line 2 large baking trays with non-stick baking paper.

Using a 6cm round cookie cutter, cut 20 rounds from the dough, re-rolling as necessary. Place on the trays and bake for 12–15 minutes or until golden and crisp. Allow to cool on the trays for 5 minutes. Transfer to wire racks to cool completely before serving. MAKES 20

currant, juniper and blue cheese biscuits

1 x quantity basic parmesan biscuit dough (see *recipe*, above)
1 tablespoon juniper berries
50g firm blue cheese, crumbled
¼ cup (40g) dried currants

Follow the basic parmesan biscuit dough recipe, adding the juniper berries with the parmesan. Once the mixture comes together in the food processor, add the blue cheese and currants and pulse until just combined. Roll the dough out and refrigerate as directed.

Preheat oven to 180°C (350°F). Line 2 large baking trays with non-stick baking paper.

Using an 8cm round cookie cutter, cut 16 rounds from the dough, re-rolling as necessary. Place on the trays and bake for 12–15 minutes or until golden and crisp. Allow to cool on the trays for 5 minutes. Transfer to wire racks to cool completely before serving. MAKES 16

parmesan, fennel and lemon thyme biscuits

1 x quantity basic parmesan biscuit dough (see *recipe*, left)
2 teaspoons fennel seeds
2 tablespoons lemon thyme leaves

Follow the basic parmesan biscuit dough recipe, adding the fennel seeds and thyme with the egg yolk. Roll the dough out and refrigerate as directed.

Preheat oven to 180°C (350°F). Line 2 large baking trays with non-stick baking paper. Using a 7.5cm round cookie cutter, cut 16 rounds from the dough, re-rolling as necessary. Place on the trays and bake for 12–15 minutes or until golden and crisp. Allow to cool on the trays for 5 minutes. Transfer to wire racks to cool completely before serving. MAKES 16

three-cheese biscuits

1 x quantity basic parmesan biscuit dough (see *recipe*, left)
⅓ cup (40g) finely grated cheddar
⅔ cup (80g) finely grated gruyère
1 tablespoon iced water, extra
½ cup (40g) finely grated parmesan, extra

Follow the basic parmesan biscuit dough recipe, adding the cheddar and half the gruyère with the oats. Add the extra iced water with the egg yolk. Roll the dough out and refrigerate as directed.

Preheat oven to 180°C (350°F). Line 3 large baking trays with non-stick baking paper.

Using a 5cm round cookie cutter, cut 30 rounds from the dough, re-rolling as necessary. Place on the trays and sprinkle with the remaining gruyère and extra parmesan. Bake for 12–15 minutes or until golden and crisp. Allow to cool on the trays for 5 minutes. Transfer to wire racks to cool completely before serving. MAKES 30

parmesan and pink peppercorn biscuits

2 teaspoons pink peppercorns
1 x quantity basic parmesan biscuit dough
   (see *recipe*, page 253)
2 teaspoons cracked black pepper

Place the pink peppercorns in a mortar and grind with
a pestle until finely crushed. Follow the basic parmesan
biscuit dough recipe. After rolling out the dough, remove
the top sheet of paper and sprinkle with both the peppers.
Return the paper to the dough and gently roll again to
secure. Refrigerate for 30 minutes.
   Preheat oven to 180°C (350°F). Line 2 large baking
trays with non-stick baking paper.
   Using a 6cm round cookie cutter, cut 20 rounds from
the dough, re-rolling as necessary. Place on the trays and
bake for 12–15 minutes or until golden and crisp. Allow to
cool on the trays for 5 minutes. Transfer to wire racks to
cool completely before serving. MAKES 20

wholemeal poppy seed lavosh

1 teaspoon dry yeast
⅔ cup (160ml) lukewarm water
1 teaspoon caster (superfine) sugar
1½ cups (225g) wholemeal (whole-wheat) plain
   (all-purpose) flour
2 tablespoons poppy seeds
1 teaspoon sea salt flakes, plus extra for sprinkling
¼ cup (60ml) extra virgin olive oil, plus extra for brushing

Place the yeast, water and sugar in a small bowl and mix
to combine. Set aside in a warm place for 5–10 minutes
or until the surface is foamy.
   Place the flour, poppy seeds and salt in a large bowl and
mix to combine. Make a well in the centre and add the oil
and the yeast mixture. Mix until a dough forms. Turn the
dough out and knead for 5–6 minutes or until smooth and
elastic. Place in a large lightly oiled bowl, cover and set
aside in a warm place for 20 minutes or until risen slightly.
   Preheat oven to 180°C (350°F). Line 2 large baking
trays with non-stick baking paper.
   Roll the dough out on a lightly floured surface to 1mm
thick. Using both 6.5cm and 7.5cm leaf-shaped cutters,
cut 40 leaves from the dough. Place half the leaves on
the trays. Brush with the extra oil, sprinkle with the
extra salt and bake for 10–12 minutes or until puffed and
golden brown. Transfer to wire racks and repeat with the
remaining shapes, extra oil and salt. Allow to cool before
serving. MAKES 40

wholemeal poppy seed lavosh

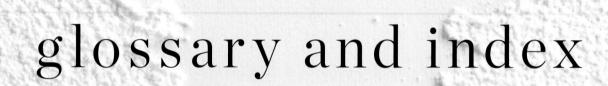

glossary and index

In the glossary, you'll find basic information on pantry staples, plus notes on any of the unusual ingredients called for in this book. There are also some really useful pages of global measures, temperatures, weights and common conversions. Find all recipes listed alphabetically by name in the index, as well as grouped by their main ingredients.

almond meal (ground almonds)

Take care not to confuse this popular baking ingredient with almond flour, which has a much finer texture. Available at most supermarkets, or make your own by processing whole almonds to a meal in a food processor: 125g almonds should give 1 cup of almond meal.

baking powder

A raising agent used in baking, consisting of bicarbonate of soda and/or cream of tartar. Most are gluten free (check the labels). Baking powder that is kept beyond its use-by date can often lose effectiveness. To create a makeshift self-raising (self-rising) flour, add 2 teaspoons of baking powder to each 1 cup (150g) of plain (all-purpose) flour and sift repeatedly to combine.

bay leaves

These aromatic leaves of the bay tree are available both fresh from some greengrocers and dried from the spice section of supermarkets. Add to soups, stews and stocks for a savoury depth of flavour. Remove before serving.

bicarbonate of (baking) soda

Also known as baking soda, bicarbonate of soda (sodium bicarbonate) is an alkaline powder used to help leaven baked goods and neutralise acids. It's also often hailed as having multiple uses around the home, notably as an effective cleaner.

black sea salt flakes

Naturally coloured with carbon or charcoal, black sea salt flakes are interchangeable with regular sea salt flakes. Find them at specialty grocers and most supermarkets.

blue swimmer crab

A common edible crab named for its vibrant blue-coloured shell. Available green (raw) and cooked from fish shops and markets. Ask your fishmonger to cut and clean the crab if necessary, and eat on the day of purchase.

breadcrumbs

To make breadcrumbs, cut and discard the crusts from 2 slices (140g) stale white or sourdough bread. Tear the bread into pieces and place in a food processor. Pulse into either coarse or fine crumbs. MAKES 1 CUP

bao buns

Also known as steamed buns, these fluffy cloud-like buns originate from Asian cuisines and are often served during yum cha. They're usually warmed up and filled with meat, seafood and vegetables, then served as a starter. You can make your own or find them at some supermarkets or Asian grocers.

brioche slider buns

Soft and light with a glossy exterior, these small French-style brioche rolls are perfect for making mini burgers or lobster rolls. Find them at bakeries, greengrocers and most supermarkets.

broccolini (tenderstem)

Also known as tenderstem broccoli, broccolini is a cross between gai lan (Chinese broccoli) and broccoli. Sold in bunches, it can be substituted for regular heads of broccoli.

butter

Unless stated otherwise in a recipe, butter should be at room temperature for cooking. It should not be half-melted or too soft to handle. We use unsalted butter in most recipes but you can use regular salted butter if you prefer.

cashew butter

Widely considered to be a healthier alternative to peanut butter thanks to its naturally lower sodium content and high vitamin, protein and mineral count, cashew butter is made from roasted, crushed and blended cashew nuts. Available at most supermarkets, it's used as a spread or to give sweet treats a creamy, nutty hit.

cheese

cream

A fresh, salted, spreadable cheese sold in tubs or foil-wrapped blocks. Mostly used as a spread for sandwiches and bagels or as the base for cream cheese frosting that tops carrot cakes and muffins.

goat's cheese

Goat's milk has a tart flavour, so the cheese made from it, also called chèvre, has a sharp, slightly acidic taste. Immature goat's cheese is mild and creamy and is often labelled goat's curd, which is spreadable. Mature goat's cheese is available in both hard and soft varieties.

gruyère

A firm cow's milk cheese with a smooth ivory interior and a natural brushed rind. Popular in Switzerland as a table cheese and cooked into fondues, gratins and quiches. It makes a fabulous melting cheese, especially in toasted sandwiches.

mascarpone

A fresh Italian triple-cream curd-style cheese, mascarpone has a smooth consistency, similar to thick (double) cream. Available in tubs from delis and most supermarkets, it's used in sauces and desserts such as tiramisu, as well as in icings and frostings for its luscious creaminess and subtle tang.

mozzarella

Italian in origin, mozzarella is the mild, fresh white cheese of pizza, lasagne, salads and pastry-based starters. It's made by cutting and spinning (or stringing) the curd to achieve a smooth, elastic consistency. Types of mozzarella include bocconcini, buffalo mozzarella and burrata. Buy fresh mozzarella from supermarkets, grocers and delicatessens. Supermarkets also sell a packaged, grated mozzarella, which is usually pale yellow in colour and drier in texture.

pecorino

A popular hard Italian cheese made from sheep's milk, pecorino has a sharp flavour similar to that of parmesan cheese. Find it at delicatessens, cheese shops and most supermarkets. If unavailable, you can substitute with parmesan cheese.

ricotta

A creamy, finely grained white cheese, ricotta means 'recooked' in Italian, a reference to the way the cheese is produced by heating the whey left over from making other cheeses. Fresh full-cream and low-fat ricotta is available at the deli counter of supermarkets. The recipes in this book call for fresh full-cream ricotta, which works particularly well in gnocchi, cheesecakes and pancakes – don't substitute with the smoother variety that's pre-packaged in tubs.

triple cream brie

A classic soft-ripened cheese with a white edible rind and a minimum butter fat content of 60%. It has all the subtle characteristics of brie but with a smoother, creamier texture. Find it at most supermarkets, delis or cheesemongers.

chickpeas (garbanzo beans)

If not ground into besan flour, these legumes are used whole in soups and stews or blended to make hummus. Dried chickpeas must be soaked beforehand, while canned chickpeas can just be rinsed and drained.

chocolate

dark

The dark chocolate called for in this book contains 70% cocoa solids and is labelled as such. It has a more bitter, intense flavour with a slightly powdery texture, ideal for use in baking and desserts that call for richness.

melted

To melt chocolate, place the required amount of chopped chocolate in a heatproof bowl over a saucepan of simmering water (the bowl shouldn't touch the water). Stir until smooth.

milk

Sweet and smooth, with a paler colour than dark chocolate, milk chocolate is the most popular for eating. It usually contains around 25% cocoa solids.

white

Made from cocoa butter and milk solids, white chocolate is super sweet and creamy in colour.

coconut

desiccated

The flesh of coconuts which has been shredded and dried, desiccated coconut is unsweetened and quite powdery.

flakes

Shaved from coconut flesh and dried, these thin flakes are sweet with a chewy texture. Used for decorating cakes and in baking or muesli. You can toast them in the oven until golden.

shredded

Coarser than desiccated coconut, shredded coconut is perfect for adding a moreish chewy texture to slices and cookies.

coriander (cilantro)

This aromatic green herb is also called cilantro. The delicate leaves have a signature flavour and, sometimes along with the finely chopped roots and stems, are commonly used in Asian and Mexican cooking.

coriander seeds

These dried seeds of the coriander plant are sold ground or whole and are one of the base ingredients in curry. They're different to (and cannot be substituted with) the fresh leaves.

cream

The fat content of these different varieties of creams determines their names and uses.

crème fraîche

A rich, tangy, fermented cream, traditionally from France, crème fraîche has a minimum fat content of 35%. It's available at grocers, delicatessens and most supermarkets.

double (thick)

Often called heavy, or dollop, cream, double cream has a butter fat content of 40–50%. It's usually served as a side with warm puddings, pies and rich cakes.

pure cream

With a butter fat content of 20–30%, this thin cream is the variety most commonly used in savoury cooking, and desserts like ice-cream, panna cotta and custard. It can be whipped to a light and airy consistency. It's also called single or whipping cream.

sour

A fermented cream with a minimum fat content of 35%, sour cream is readily available in supermarkets and used for its creamy-yet-tangy flavour.

crystallised ginger

Crystallised ginger gives cookies and slices a warm spicy flavour with a sweet finish. The firm, dried ginger pieces, coated in sugar, are available in supermarkets and health food stores.

cumin seeds

This ancient spice, from a plant of the parsley family, is common in Middle-Eastern and Indian cooking. The small long brown seeds are peppery and aromatic with distinct flavour, particularly when toasted. Buy cumin seeds, whole or ground, from the spice section of supermarkets.

dulce de leche

This thick milk caramel, common in Latin American desserts, is made by slowly heating and thickening sweetened milk. Buy good-quality ready-made versions from supermarkets and grocers or make your own by gently boiling an unopened can (not a ring-pull can) of sweetened condensed milk for 2–3 hours. Use as a rich caramel filling for tarts, a topping on cakes, or drizzled over ice-cream.

eggs

The standard egg size used in this book is 60g. It is important to use the right-sized eggs for a recipe, as this will affect the outcome of baked goods. This is especially important when using eggwhites to make meringues. Use eggs at room temperature for baking, and use the mantra 'fresh is best' when it comes to choosing your eggs.

eschalots (french shallots)

A member of the onion family, eschalots are smaller and have a milder flavour than brown, red or white onions. Used frequently in European cooking, they look like small elongated brown onions with purple and beige skins – not to be confused with green or spring onions.

fennel seeds

The green seeds of the common fennel plant impart a warm anise note to breads and chutneys as well as fish, meat and vegetable dishes. Toast and/or grind them for maximum flavour.

flour

00 (superfine)

Graded '00' for its texture via the Italian milling system, this superfine flour makes for soft and stretchy dough and is used for making pizza, pasta and desserts. Available from the baking aisle of most supermarkets.

cornflour (cornstarch)

When made from ground corn or maize, cornflour is gluten free. It's quite often blended with water or stock to be used as a thickening agent. Not to be confused with cornflour in the United States, which is finely ground corn meal.

plain (all-purpose)

Ground from the endosperm of wheat, plain white flour contains no raising agent.

rice

Rice flour is a fine flour made from ground rice. Available in white and brown varieties, it's often used as a thickening agent in baking, in cookies and shortbreads, and to coat foods when cooking Asian dishes like crispy tofu or tempura.

self-raising (self-rising)

Ground from the endosperm of wheat, self-raising flour contains raising agents including sodium carbonates and calcium phosphates. To make it using plain flour, add 2 teaspoons of baking powder to every 1 cup (150g) of flour.

spelt

Milled from the ancient cereal grain, spelt flour boasts more nutrients and is better tolerated by some than regular flour. White spelt flour is easier to bake with, while wholemeal has more of the grain's goodness. It lends a warm, nutty flavour to breads and cakes. Find spelt flour in the health aisle of supermarkets.

wholemeal (whole-wheat)

Ground from the whole grain of wheat and thus keeping more of its nutrients and fibre, this flour is available in plain (all-purpose) and self-raising (self-rising) varieties from most supermarkets and health food stores. It gives pasta, breads, cakes and baked goods a unique body and flavour.

golden syrup

Also known as light treacle, this thick, dark amber-coloured syrup is made from sugar and water. It's used to impart a deep toffee-caramel flavour to sweets and desserts. If it's not available, use maple syrup instead.

horseradish

A pungent root vegetable that releases mustard oil when cut or grated, horseradish oxidises quickly, so use it immediately after cutting or cover with water or vinegar. Fresh horseradish is preferable – find it at greengrocers. You can also buy it ready-grated or as horseradish cream in jars from the supermarket.

juniper berries
The aromatic and bitter dried berries of a hardy evergreen bush, juniper is used for pickling vegetables, flavouring sauces and, most famously, for infusing gin. It offers a great savoury kick.

liquid glucose
Liquid glucose is used in the making of confectionery such as hard candy, marshmallow and jellies. Find it in the baking aisle of supermarkets.

maple syrup
A sweetener made from the sap of the maple tree. Be sure to use pure maple syrup rather than imitation or maple-flavoured pancake syrup.

marjoram
A delicately flavoured herb, related to mint and very similar in flavour to oregano.

micro herbs
The baby version of fresh herbs, these tiny edible leaves have a great intensity of flavour despite their size. They make a beautiful garnish – sprinkle them liberally over cooked dishes or into salads, or place them onto individual canapés. Find them in small pots and in a loose mix at farmers' markets and greengrocers.

mirin (japanese rice wine)
A pale yellow Japanese cooking wine made from glutinous rice and alcohol. Sweet mirin is flavoured with corn syrup. Find it at supermarkets.

mustard
dijon
Also called French mustard, this creamy, mild-flavoured condiment originated in France. It's an important ingredient in vinaigrette.

oil
olive
Olive oil is graded according to its flavour, aroma and acidity. Extra virgin is the highest quality olive oil – it contains no more than 1% acid. Virgin is the next best – it contains 1.5% or less acid. Bottles labelled simply 'olive oil' contain a blend of refined and unrefined virgin olive oil. 'Light' olive oil is the least pure in quality and shouldn't be confused with light-flavoured extra virgin olive oil. Where possible, it's best to keep a bottle of extra virgin olive oil on-hand for everyday use in cooking and dressings, plus a light-flavoured extra virgin olive oil for baking.

sesame
Pressed from sesame seeds, sesame oil is used in Asian cuisine more as a nutty, full-flavoured seasoning than a cooking medium. It is also a popular ingredient in salad dressings. Find it in the Asian aisle of the supermarket or at Asian grocers.

vegetable
Oils sourced from plants or seeds, such as sunflower or grapeseed oil, with very mild, unobtrusive flavours. Often called for in baking recipes, like muffins or loaf cakes, or for deep-frying. It's handy to keep a bottle of all-purpose oil labelled simply 'vegetable oil' on-hand in your pantry.

pancetta
This cured and rolled Italian-style pork is similar to prosciutto, but less salty and with a softer texture. It's sold in flat pieces or chunks, or is thinly sliced into rounds. You can also ask your butcher to slice it for you. Pancetta lends stuffing mixtures a salty, savoury kick. Find it at supermarkets, Italian delicatessens and butchers.

paprika
smoked
Unlike Hungarian paprika, the Spanish style known as pimentón is deep and smoky in flavour. It is made from smoked, ground pimento peppers and comes in varying intensities from sweet and mild (dulce), bittersweet medium hot (agridulce) to hot (picante).

sweet
Made from dried, ground red capsicums (peppers), this earthy coloured powder is used as a spice, seasoning and garnish.

pastry
Make your own or use one of the many store-bought varieties, which are sold frozen in blocks or ready-rolled into sheets. Defrost in the fridge before use.

filo (phyllo)
Extremely thin sheets of pastry, popular in Turkish, Greek and Middle-Eastern baking. Each sheet is usually brushed with oil or melted butter and then layered, before encasing a filling. Keep sheets from drying out while working by covering with a clean damp tea towel. Find it in the fridge or freezer section of the supermarket.

puff and butter puff
This pastry is quite difficult to make, so many cooks opt to use store-bought puff pastry. It can be bought in blocks from patisseries, or is sold in both block and sheet forms in supermarkets. Butter puff pastry is light and flaky, perfect for sweet pies and tarts. Often labelled as 'all butter puff', good-quality sheets are usually thicker. If you can only find thin sheets, don't be afraid to stack 2 regular thawed sheets together.

shortcrust

Shortcrust pastry is a savoury or sweet pastry that is available ready-made in blocks and frozen sheets. Keep a supply in the freezer for last-minute pies, or make your own:

1½ cups (225g) plain (all-purpose) flour
125g cold unsalted butter, chopped
3 egg yolks
1 tablespoon iced water

Place the flour and butter in a food processor and process in short bursts until the mixture resembles fine breadcrumbs. While the motor is running, add the egg yolks and water. Process until a dough just comes together. Turn out the dough onto a lightly floured surface and gently bring together to form a ball. Flatten the dough into a disc, wrap in plastic wrap and refrigerate for 30 minutes or until firm. When ready to use, roll out on a lightly floured surface to 3mm thick. To make sweet shortcrust pastry, add ½ cup (80g) icing (confectioner's) sugar.

pedro ximénez sherry

Pedro Ximénez sherry, or PX, is an intensely sweet, dark dessert sherry made from the Spanish grape variety of the same name that lends depth to desserts such as trifles, that call for soaking of biscuits or cake. It's available in liquor stores.

pink peppercorns

While not technically peppercorns, these dried berries still have a mild, peppery warmth to them with slightly sweet notes. Lending their pretty, rosy colour to dishes, they're perfect cracked over chicken, fish or canapés. Buy them at most supermarkets, delis and spice shops.

prosciutto

Italian ham that's been salted and dried for up to 2 years. The paper-thin slices are eaten raw in salads or over savoury pastries, or used to lend their distinctive flavour to braises and other cooked dishes. It's sometimes used to wrap around vegetables for extra flavour and great presentation.

puffed brown rice

Whole grains of rice are heated and pressured to puff into a light, aerated cereal. Great as part of a muesli blend or baked into treats. Find them in the health food aisle of the supermarket and at health food shops.

quince jelly

Find quince jelly in the jam or relish aisles of major supermarkets, or at specialty grocers and delicatessens.

sesame seeds

These small glossy seeds have a creamy, nutty flavour and can be used in savoury and sweet cooking. White sesame seeds are the most common variety, but black, or unhulled, seeds are popular for coatings in Asian cooking as well as some Asian desserts.

shiso leaves

Sometimes called perilla, this herb comes in both green and purple-leafed varieties. It has a slight peppery flavour and can be used to wrap ingredients. The micro (baby) variety makes a pretty garnish. Find it at some greengrocers and Asian markets.

sour cherries

This book calls for both frozen and dried pitted sour cherries. Find them, sometimes labelled as 'tart' cherries, at major supermarkets, greengrocers and specialty grocers.

sponge finger biscuits

Sweet and light Italian finger-shaped biscuits, also known as savoiardi. Great for desserts such as tiramisu because they absorb other flavours and soften well, yet at the same time maintain their shape. Available in both large and small versions at supermarkets.

star-anise

A small brown seed cluster that is shaped like a star. It has a strong aniseed flavour and can be used whole or ground in sweet and savoury dishes. It works well in master stocks or braises.

streaky bacon

Also known as American-style bacon or belly bacon, streaky bacon is from the back end of the pork loin. Cured and smoked, it's sold in thin strips or slices and can now be found in most supermarkets and at specialty grocers.

sugar

Extracted as crystals from the juice of the sugarcane plant or beet, sugar is a sweetener, flavour enhancer, bulking agent and preservative.

brown

Light and dark brown sugars are made from refined sugar with natural molasses added. The molasses gives a smooth caramel flavour and a soft texture. Both varieties are available at supermarkets. When measuring out for recipes in this book, be sure to firmly pack it into the cup.

caster (superfine)

The most commonly called for sugar in this book, caster sugar gives baked goods a light texture and delicate crumb, thanks to its fine grain. Used in many cakes as well as airy desserts such as meringues, it dissolves easily.

coffee sugar crystals
With its full-bodied caramel flavour, golden honey hue and easy-to-dissolve composition, this sugar is used in sweets, such as caramels, or in desserts where a deep caramel flavour is desired. Find it at most supermarkets or online.

demerara
This sugar's large crystals, with their golden colour and mild caramel flavour, give baked goods a pronounced crust, and coffee a distinct flavour.

icing (confectioner's)
A granulated sugar ground to a very fine powder. When mixed with liquid or into butter or cream cheese it creates a sweet glaze or icing, or it can be sifted over cakes. Unless specified, use pure icing sugar, not icing sugar mixture, which contains cornflour (cornstarch) and needs more liquid.

rapadura
Made by crushing sugar cane stalks to extract and then evaporate the juice, this variety of brown cane sugar is typically high in molasses, which gives it a deep caramel colour and flavour. Unrefined rapadura is preferable.

white (granulated)
Regular granulated sugar is used in baking when a light texture is not crucial. The crystals are larger, so you need to beat, add liquids or heat to dissolve them.

tahini
A thick paste made from ground sesame seeds. Used in Middle-Eastern cooking and to make the dip hummus, it's available in jars and cans from supermarkets and health food shops. Recipes in this book call for the hulled variety, for its smoother texture.

vanilla
bean paste
This store-bought paste is a convenient way to replace whole vanilla beans and is great in desserts. 1 teaspoon of paste substitutes for 1 vanilla bean. Find it in small jars or tubes in the baking aisle of most supermarkets.

beans
These fragrant cured pods from the vanilla orchid are used whole, often split with the tiny seeds inside scraped into the mixture, to infuse flavour into custard and cream-based recipes. They offer a rich and rounded vanilla flavour.

extract
Syrup-like and readily available from the baking aisle of supermarkets, choose a good-quality vanilla extract, not an essence or imitation flavour.

vincotto
Translating literally as 'cooked wine', vincotto is a syrup made from grapes with a sharp, sweet-sour flavour. Use it as you would balsamic vinegar. Find it in supermarkets, delicatessens and specialty grocers.

vinegar
apple cider
Made from apple must, cider vinegar has a golden amber hue and a sour appley flavour. Use it in dressings, marinades and chutneys. It offers a delicate fruity acidity when used in ham glazes.

balsamic
Originally from Modena in Italy, there are many varieties of balsamic vinegar, ranging in quality and flavour. Aged balsamics are generally preferable. Also available in a milder white version, made with white, as opposed to red, wine.

malt
Produced from ale made from malted barley, this vinegar is typically light brown in colour. Used in pickles and chutneys, or in glazes for hams, it's traditionally thought of as a natural partner for fish and chips.

rice wine
Made from fermenting rice or rice wine, rice vinegar is milder and sweeter than the vinegars made by oxidising distilled alcohol or wine made from grapes. Available in white, black and red varieties from Asian food stores and some supermarkets.

white
A strong, everyday vinegar made from distilled grain alcohol.

wine
Both red and white wine can be distilled into vinegar for use in dressings, glazes, sauces and preserved condiments such as pickles. This is the vinegar to use in the classic French dressing, vinaigrette.

yeast
Dry yeast, sometimes called active dry yeast, is a granular raising agent primarily used to make dough for breads, pizzas and sweet baked treats such as doughnuts. Buy it in sachets from the supermarket.

yoghurt
plain thick
A fridge staple, natural, unsweetened, full-fat Greek-style (thick) yoghurt has multiple uses in the kitchen, from dressings to baked goods and desserts. Buy it from the chilled section of the supermarket, checking the label for any unwanted added sweeteners or artificial flavours.

global measures

───○───

Measures vary from Europe
to the US and even from
Australia to New Zealand.

metric and imperial

Measuring cups and spoons may
vary slightly from one country
to another, but the difference is
generally not sufficient to affect
a recipe. The recipes in this book
use Australian measures. All cup
and spoon measures are level.
An Australian measuring cup holds
250ml (8 fl oz).

One Australian metric teaspoon
holds 5ml, one Australian tablespoon
holds 20ml (4 teaspoons). However,
in North America, New Zealand
and the UK, 15ml (3-teaspoon)
tablespoons are used.

When measuring liquid ingredients,
remember that 1 American pint
contains 500ml (16 fl oz) but
1 imperial pint contains
600ml (20 fl oz).

When measuring dry ingredients, add
the ingredient loosely to the cup and
level with a knife. Don't tap or shake
to compact the ingredient unless
the recipe requests 'firmly packed'.

When measuring a tin, dish or tray,
always measure across the base,
from edge to edge (the diameter).

liquids and solids

───○───

Measuring cups, spoons
and a set of scales are great
assets in the kitchen.

liquids

cup	metric	imperial
⅛ cup	30ml	1 fl oz
¼ cup	60ml	2 fl oz
⅓ cup	80ml	2½ fl oz
½ cup	125ml	4 fl oz
⅔ cup	160ml	5 fl oz
¾ cup	180ml	6 fl oz
1 cup	250ml	8 fl oz
2 cups	500ml	16 fl oz
2¼ cups	560ml	20 fl oz
4 cups	1 litre	32 fl oz

solids

metric	imperial
20g	½ oz
60g	2 oz
125g	4 oz
180g	6 oz
250g	8 oz
500g	16 oz (1lb)
1kg	32 oz (2lb)

more equivalents

───○───

Here are some equivalents for
metric and imperial measures,
plus varying ingredient names.

millimetres to inches

metric	imperial
3mm	⅛ inch
6mm	¼ inch
1cm	½ inch
2.5cm	1 inch
5cm	2 inches
18cm	7 inches
20cm	8 inches
23cm	9 inches
25cm	10 inches
30cm	12 inches

ingredient equivalents

almond meal	ground almonds
bicarbonate of soda	baking soda
capsicum	bell pepper
caster sugar	superfine sugar
celeriac	celery root
chickpeas	garbanzo beans
coriander	cilantro
cornflour	cornstarch
cos lettuce	romaine lettuce
eggplant	aubergine
gai lan	chinese broccoli
green onion	scallion
icing sugar	confectioner's sugar
plain flour	all-purpose flour
rocket	arugula
self-raising flour	self-rising flour
snow pea	mange tout
white sugar	granulated sugar
zucchini	courgette

oven temperatures

─○─

Setting the oven to the right
temperature can be crucial
when baking sweet things.

oven settings

All our recipes are created and tested
in fan-forced electric ovens. If using
a conventional (non fan-forced) oven,
increase the temperature by 20°C.

celsius to fahrenheit

celsius	fahrenheit
100°C	200°F
120°C	250°F
140°C	275°F
150°C	300°F
160°C	325°F
180°C	350°F
190°C	375°F
200°C	400°F
220°C	425°F

electric to gas

celsius	gas
110°C	¼
130°C	½
140°C	1
150°C	2
170°C	3
180°C	4
190°C	5
200°C	6
220°C	7
230°C	8
240°C	9
250°C	10

butter and eggs

─○─

Let 'fresh is best' be your
mantra when it comes to
selecting eggs and dairy goods.

butter

We generally use unsalted
butter as it allows for a little more
control over a recipe's flavour.
Either way, the impact is minimal.
Salted butter has a longer shelf life
and is preferred by some people.
One American stick of butter is
125g (4 oz). One Australian block
of butter is 250g (8 oz).

eggs

Unless otherwise indicated, we use
large (60g) chicken eggs. To preserve
freshness, store eggs in the refrigerator
in the carton they are sold in. Use only
the freshest eggs in recipes such as
mayonnaise or dressings that use raw or
barely cooked eggs. Be extra cautious if
there is a salmonella problem in your
community, particularly in food that
is to be served to children, pregnant
women or the elderly.

useful weights

─○─

Here are a few simple weight
conversions for cupfuls of
commonly used ingredients.

common ingredients

almond meal (ground almonds)
1 cup | 120g
brown sugar
1 cup | 240g
white (granulated) sugar
1 cup | 220g
caster (superfine) sugar
1 cup | 220g
icing (confectioner's) sugar
1 cup | 160g
cocoa
1 cup | 100g
plain (all-purpose)
or self-raising (self-rising) flour
1 cup | 150g
wholemeal (whole-wheat) spelt flour
1 cup | 120g
fresh breadcrumbs
1 cup | 70g
finely grated parmesan
1 cup | 80g
shelled pistachios
1 cup | 150g
fresh or frozen berries
1 cup | 125g
honey
1 cup | 360g

I know for a fact that Christmas came early for a few people this year – my dream team!
In my studio, we've been busily tasting everything from turkey to trifle for months now
(plus more gingerbread cookies than we care to count). I'm beyond grateful for their
dedication. Special mention must go to the incredible Chi, creative director of this book;
Hannah Schubert, my wonderful wing woman and art director; and to Abby and Mariam,
my amazing editors. At HarperCollins*Publishers*, Jim, Catherine, Janelle and Belinda,
thank you for making this possible – I so appreciate your ongoing support.
Lastly, to my friends and family (especially Angus and Tom), thank you for all your love.
Despite this cheeky head start, I honestly can't wait to share my Christmas with you.

About Donna

As Australia's *leading food editor* and *best-selling cookbook author*, Donna Hay has made her way into the hearts (and *almost every home*) across the country.

An *international publishing phenomenon*, Donna's name is synonymous with accessible yet *inspirational recipes* and *stunning images.* Her acclaimed magazine notched up an *incredible 100* issues and her best-selling cookbooks have sold more than *eight million copies* worldwide.

The *donna hay brand* goes beyond the printed page, featuring an *impressive digital presence*; a number of *television series*; branded merchandise; and a *baking mix range* in Australian supermarkets. Donna is the *very proud mum* of two teenage boys, adores living near the ocean and *still loves cooking* every single day.

Connect with Donna anytime, anywhere...

 www.donnahay.com

 @donna.hay

 pinterest.com/donnahayhome

 facebook.com/donnahay